D1277679

Brokered Homeland

The Anthropology of Contemporary Issues

A Series Edited by

ROGER SANJEK

A full list of titles in the series appears at the end of this book.

Brokered Homeland

Japanese Brazilian Migrants in Japan

JOSHUA HOTAKA ROTH

CORNELL UNIVERSITY PRESS

Ithaca & London

Copyright © 2002 by Cornell University

All rights reserved. Except for brief quotations in a review, this book, or parts thereof, must not be reproduced in any form without permission in writing from the publisher. For information, address Cornell University Press, Sage House, 512 East State Street, Ithaca, New York 14850.

First published 2002 by Cornell University Press
First printing, Cornell Paperbacks, 2002

Printed in the United States of America

Library of Congress Cataloging-in-Publication Data

Roth, Joshua Hotaka.
    Brokered homeland: Japanese Brazilian migrants in Japan / Joshua
Hotaka Roth.
        p. cm. — (The anthropology of contemporary issues)
Includes bibliographical references and index.
    ISBN 978-0-8014-8808-5 (pbk. : alk. paper)
    1. Brazilians—Japan. 2. Alien labor, Brazilian—Japan. 3.
Japan—Ethnic relations.   I. Title. II. Series.
    DS832.7. B73 R68 2002
    952'.004698—dc21

                                                    2002001539

Cornell University Press strives to use environmentally responsible suppliers and materials to the fullest extent possible in the publishing of its books. Such materials include vegetable-based, low-VOC inks and acid-free papers that are recycled, totally chlorine-free, or partly composed of non-wood fibers. For further information, visit our website at www.cornellpress.cornell.edu.

Paperback printing   10   9   8   7   6   5   4   3

Contents

Acknowledgments

I am most grateful to the Brazilians and Japanese who allowed me to take part in their lives, guided me in my research, and in the process enriched my own life so much. I thank them for helping me with their languages, both Portuguese and Japanese, and for teaching me to samba and to fly kites. I could not have completed this research without their patience and confidence. Most will not be able to recognize more than bits and pieces of themselves, but their stories, wisdom, and friendship inform much of this work. I must give special thanks to Edgar Date, the Fujita family, Carlos Goke, Amelia Higa, Hugo Higuchi, Rosângela Iwase, the Kato family, Miriam Kohatsu, Kondo Eiji,[1] Kondo Rumi, Maurício Miyamoto, Sandra Nishihara, Nelson Omachi, Terumi Ota, the Saito family, Hélio Sato, the Shima family, the Shinkai family, Suzuki Yasuyuki, Mariko Tome, Carlos Tsujimoto, and Paulo Yamazaki for bringing me into their worlds. Gerard Adam, Ikeda Kunitoshi, Monna Kunio, Nojima Hiroyuki, Ogawa Tadao, Sasaki Tadao, Takeuchi Yasuto, and other members of the Hamamatsu Overseas Laborers Solidarity stimulated me in thinking about workplace issues. Thanks go to the Okuno family, Sugiyama-san, Takeyama-sensei, and other members of the Hokubu community center's Batepapo group, and to Mokuya Noriko, Ken Shima, and members of the Nanbu community center's Portuguese language class. Fujiwaki Chinatsu, Kimata Keigo, Kimura Motomi (whom we will remember fondly), Matsuura Chisato, Matsuura

---

[1] Japanese names are written with family name first unless citing a person known primarily through articles published in English with the order of names reversed.

Naoki, Edivaldo de Oliveira Santos (a.k.a. Bada), Suzuki Mitsuko, and other members of Sambeaba played with an enthusiasm that was infectious. Any shortcomings in the writing and in my samba are my sole responsibility.

Preliminary fieldwork during the summer of 1992 was funded by an Einaudi Center Summer Research Travel Grant, Cornell University. Portuguese language training during the summer of 1993 was made possible through a Peace Studies Summer Study Grant and a Sage Graduate Center Summer Study Grant, both from Cornell University. The bulk of the fieldwork during 1994 and 1995 was supported by a grant from the Japan Foundation. Follow-up research during the summer of 1997 was made possible by an East Asia Program Summer Research Travel Grant, Cornell University.

Robert J. Smith's pioneering work in the anthropology of Japan and his early work with Japanese Brazilians helped me conceive my project, and he has been a constant source of encouragement. John Borneman, Davydd Greenwood, Victor Koschmann, and Maeyama Takashi all provided constructive criticism during both research and write-up stages.

Ted Bestor, Michelle Bigenho, Jeffrey Lesser, Daniel Linger, Lorna Rhodes, Steve Rubenstein, Katherine Tegtmeyer Pak, and Barbara Yngvesson provided me with helpful comments on various chapters. At the early stage of writing, John Borneman organized a cohort of scholars at Cornell into a group that provided me with an abundance of stimulating commentary. Members of that group included Thamora Fishel, John Norvell, Lazima Onta, Stefan Senders, Pat Walker, Amrih Widodo, Erick White, Jan Zeserson, and Li Zhang. The creativity and rigor of their research projects inspired me in my own.

I have had great encouragement from colleagues and friends in anthropology, Japanese studies, and related fields. Among them I would like to thank George Allinson, Eyal Ben-Ari, Wayne Cornelius, Fukuoka Yasunori, Susan Hanley, Steve Harrell, Naoto Higuchi, Hosokawa Shūhei, Ikegami Noriaki, Angelo Ishi, Anne Kaneko, Charles Keyes, Kitagawa Toyoie, Kuwahara Yasuo, Takie Lebra, Mori Kōichi, Gordon Mathews, Robert North, Ōtsuka Chie, Glenda Roberts, Jennifer Robertson, Steve Sangren, Pat Steinhoff, Tanaka Hiroshi, John Treat, Gaku Tsuda, Keiko Yamanaka, Karen Yamashita, Yamawaki Keizō, and Kathleen Zane.

My colleagues at Mount Holyoke College have provided me with a stimulating environment in which to develop my ideas. Thanks go especially to Debbora Battaglia, Andrew Lass, Jonathan Lipman, Lynn Morgan, Naoko Nemoto, Indira Peterson, Eleanor Townsley, Ken Tucker, Ying Wang, and Tada Yamashita.

At Cornell University Press, my thanks go to Roger Sanjek and to an anonymous reader who provided useful guidance about how to highlight my major points. Fran Benson was crucial in shepherding the manuscript through to publication.

Beth Notar has read the roughest drafts of all my chapters, saving me from embarrassment in front of wider audiences. Her encouragement, as well as the example of her own research and writing, has motivated me since the earliest days of my project.

To my parents, Richard and Ikuko Roth, I owe a debt that cannot be repaid. Not only did they provide me with a comfortable home for so many years; they also demonstrated a creative, adventurous, and tenacious spirit in their careers that has been a source of inspiration for me. Hi to my brother Abe.

[1]

Introduction

I have a few vivid memories of the years I lived in Japan with my brother and parents between the ages of two and four. I remember visiting my grandparents at their home in Kunitachi, Tokyo. I remember visiting *Kunitachi obāsan* (Grandmother in Kunitachi) in the hospital and later playing with my mother's prayer beads while the monk chanted during a long Buddhist funeral. I remember our neighbor's overgrown backyard that extended down a steep hillside, and the thousands of snails that would magically emerge in that backyard after a rain. A sinking feeling would overcome me when I crushed some underfoot despite my best efforts to avoid them. I remember my bright yellow plastic umbrella.

Expectations of Self-understanding

I returned to Japan in 1988—almost twenty years later—influenced by a mixture of opportunities and constraints. Unable to find interesting work in New York City after graduating from college, I was lured to Tokyo by lucrative teaching opportunities. But I was also drawn in a subdued way by the scattered images of a distant childhood, by curiosity about my mother's side of my family, about my roots, and ultimately about myself. This underlying expectation of self-revelation was something I shared with other *Nikkeijin* (Japanese and their descendants residing overseas) in our travels to Japan.

As it turned out, these expectations of self-understanding fulfilled themselves in unexpected ways. At the time, I did not identify myself as Japanese American, but rather as someone whose mother happened to be Japanese. Since then, I have come to think of myself as Nikkeijin, partly as a result of my identification with the Japanese Brazilians I got to know during my research.

One of them, Marcelo Matsumoto, was studying for a master's degree in agriculture in 1988 when I met him. His father had been born and raised in Hyōgo Prefecture before immigrating to Brazil in 1960 to work as an agronomist. Many Japanese prefectures offered scholarships to Nikkeijin whose parents or grandparents were from those prefectures. Marcelo had applied for and received such a scholarship to study at Kobe University, Hyōgo Prefecture's premier public institution of higher learning. After graduation, he returned to Brazil to work for a Japanese seed company in the town of Atibáia, one hour from São Paulo. Since then, his father has retired from agronomy and has taken up Japanese-style massage therapy and acupuncture, working in a small clinic in São Paulo.

Four or five other *kempi ryūgakusei* (prefectural scholarship foreign students) were living in the foreign students' dormitory at Kobe University, studying topics that ranged from nursing to business to architecture. All of these prefectural scholarship students were Japanese Brazilians. In addition, a Japanese American was studying literature on a Ministry of Education (*mombushō*) scholarship. I, myself, audited classes in anthropology and sociology.

Ironically, some Japanese Brazilians who have gone to Japan to study, and many who have gone there to work, have come to feel less a sense of belonging than they may have expected in their ancestral homeland. Some have come to think of themselves as Brazilians who happen to have Japanese parents or grandparents.

Roughly 140,000 Japanese immigrated to Brazil between 1908 and 1940, and another 60,000 immigrated there in the early postwar period. Most were second- or third-born sons and daughters who would not inherit their family land or business in Japan (Maeyama 1981). Even so, most intended to stay in Brazil only a few years and then return to Japan. War and economic difficulties made return impossible for much longer than they initially planned, however, and many established roots in Brazil as their children grew up. In the 1990s, elderly Japanese immigrants in Brazil looked back proudly on the contributions they made to Brazilian agriculture. Much of the fruit and vegetables in São Paulo's abundant street markets came from Japanese Brazilian farms in the interior of the state. Some of the largest agricultural cooperatives in Brazil were established and operated by ethnic Japanese. In the prewar era, Japanese had also established themselves as shopkeepers and small-business owners in urban areas, but starting in the 1950s more and more Japanese Brazilians moved from the countryside to the cities. Many flourished in these new surroundings, achieving

[2]

Table 1. South American Nikkeijin Registered as Residents in Japan

	1986	1988	1990	1992	1994	1996
Brazil	2,135	4,159	56,429	147,803	159,619	189,781
Peru	553	864	10,279	31,051	35,382	36,616
Argentina	359	627	2,656	3,289	2,796	3,035
Paraguay	122	282	672	1,174	1,129	1,235
Bolivia	126	150	496	2,387	2,917	2,811
Total	3,295	6,082	70,532	185,704	201,843	233,478

Source: Kaigai Nikkeijin Kyōkai 1997, 43.

high levels of education and entering a variety of professions. The total population of Japanese Brazilians has increased dramatically since the prewar era. According to one survey, they numbered more than 1.2 million in 1989 (Centro de Estudos Nipo-Brasileiros 1990).

In 1992, news of Nikkeijin migrating to Japan had become widespread in the Japanese media and had even been picked up in the *New York Times* and other Western media. I was unaware of this movement in 1989, when Marcelo and I were still at Kobe University. Nikkeijin had been going to Japan on prefectural scholarships for many years, and elderly Japanese migrants in Brazil had started to take short trips back to Japan more frequently since the 1970s, but it was not until the 1980s that Nikkeijin started traveling to Japan in great numbers to work. From 1989, economic boom in Japan and bust in Brazil motivated many Nikkeijin to take advantage of the preferred visa status the Japanese government made available for them. The dramatic rise in numbers of South American Nikkeijin registered as resident in Japan is illustrated in Table 1. Although economic conditions underlay this dramatic migration, many Nikkeijin, even those who had never been to Japan before, framed it as a return to homeland that offered the possibility of self-understanding.

Where the Bones Lie Buried

Surprisingly few Nikkeijin who went to Japan, however, ever visited their Japanese relatives. During the two years I spent doing fieldwork in Japan, I visited an unmarried uncle in a hospital once and was invited by an aunt and cousin to their house on another occasion. Subsequently, my mother and her siblings renewed long-standing arguments they had over the care of their convalescent brother, and it became awkward for me to visit my relatives. In any case, I realized that the new network of social relations I had developed in Hamamatsu, where I conducted most of my fieldwork, was far

[3]

more important to me than the connections to Japan that had existed previously. Such was the case for many younger Nikkeijin from Brazil as well. The few I knew who had visited their relatives commented that they were cold or that they seemed embarrassed to see them.

Some Japanese Brazilians said that their experiences in Japan were very different from mine because of the Japanese infatuation with all things American and their disdain for things Brazilian. Brazil's status as a Third World country in the eyes of many Japanese may have made them embarrassed to admit to having Japanese Brazilian relatives. In addition, our experiences differed because of my status as a researcher rather than an economic migrant. Nevertheless, many of us shared the experience of discovering a sense of ourselves in Japan that was based on our difference from, rather than identification with, things Japanese. If we achieved a modicum of self-understanding in our return to an ancestral homeland, it was not so much through the exploration of our roots as through a new awareness of our ties to our other homeland—Brazil or the United States—where we had lived most of our lives. Breyten Breytenbach writes of a similar experience of initial alienation and growing self-understanding upon returning to his native South Africa after many years in exile:

> Recently I went back to where the bones lie buried, and I was a stranger. My wife and I spent a night in a small-town hotel; I handed the receptionist my passport and chewed the fat with him. He congratulated me, a "foreigner," on my ability to speak the language, Afrikaans, so well—albeit, he added patronizingly, with an accent. I answered that it was surely the least a visitor could do in trying to respect the customs of a strange country.
>
> An exile never returns. "Before" does not exist for "them," the "others," those who stayed behind. For "them" it was all continuity; for you it was a fugue of disruptions. The thread is lost. The telling has shaped the story. You made your own history at the cost of not sharing theirs. The eyes, having seen too many different things, now see differently.
>
> But the return released me from exile! The crystallized shadow was cut from me. I haven't staunched the bleeding yet, but there's hope, through mourning, of a cure. Exile became a *thing* outside me, which could be discarded. I wound it up and threw it in the sky to fly. I put it to earth with the navel string, the roots and the bones. (Breytenbach 1991, 80–1; italics Breytenbach's)

The "bones" to which Breytenbach refers are the bones of his ancestors, which drew him back to South Africa. At the end of the passage he says that he is able to bury his condition of exile along "with the navel string, the roots and the bones." For Breytenbach the experience of return was liberating even if initially alienating. The alienation he felt actually helped release him from the "crystallized shadow" that the memories of his imaginary homeland had become. Return meant rebirth, not through reconnecting with the place he had come from, but rather through allowing him to bury the condition of exile he had so long experienced.

For some Japanese migrants who had lived several decades in Brazil, travel back to their homeland made the discontinuities in their lives excruciatingly explicit. Many cities had had to be rebuilt from scratch after being destroyed in firebombs during World War II. Many in a generation of young men, the companions of prewar immigrants, had died during the war. In addition to the urban centers, the villages from which many had emigrated had been transformed. Roads were paved and widened, houses rebuilt, rice paddies covered over with asphalt. Such an experience of return could have played a part in some older Japanese immigrants' resolve to "bury their bones" (*hone o umeru*) in Brazil and to become ancestors of Brazilians (Maeyama 1996b, 238; see also Roth forthcoming).

Ethnic Minority Formation in Japan

Younger Nikkeijin migrants to Japan often introduced themselves to me with an explanation like the following: "In Brazil, I'm called *'Japonês,'* and here in Japan, I'm called *'gaijin'* (foreigner). I have no home." Despite such verbal expressions of homelessness, other forms of expression suggested an increasingly strong attachment to Brazil even as they continued to live in Japan. Many who had had only a passing interest in soccer paraded with flags when Brazil won the World Cup in 1994. Many spent hundreds of dollars every month on telephone calls to friends and family in Brazil. Bootleg videotape collections proliferated and continually updated ongoing Brazilian television programs featuring news, dramas, and variety shows. Several Portuguese language newspapers were established in Japan that focused on news from Brazil as well as on Nikkeijin in Japan (see Ishi 1996). Gradually the Internet and television came to play an important role in maintaining transnational connections. Physically removed from Brazil, many Nikkeijin started to identify more strongly with Brazil in a way they had not done while living there (see Linger 2001, Tsuda 1996). Brazilian flags adorned all stores, restaurants, travel agencies, and other businesses run by or catering to Nikkeijin.

Ironically, many of these Nikkeijin who had begun to identify so strongly with Brazil appeared to be settling in Japan permanently (see Kitagawa 1993). The transnational connections that Nikkeijin have created have taken a variety of forms. For some, transnational connections have meant a literal shuttling back and forth between Japan and Brazil; for others, these connections have informed migrants' sense of place within a locality. Even

A Nikkeijin friend waits to call his family in Brazil from a store offering discount international telephone rates. A poster advertising a Japanese long-distance telephone carrier is on the wall behind him.

Celebrating Brazil's 1994 World Cup victory in downtown Hamamatsu

among those who have not decided whether to settle down in Japan, the significance of local social relationships should not be underestimated. For all the advances in communications and transportation technologies, personal worth and mental health continue to depend largely on the presence and quality of human relationships in local communities. As Ulf Hannerz has written, "People are in the local setting bodily, with all their senses" (Hannerz 1996b, 27), and electronic media have no way to convey their sense of "wooliness."[1] Such media are particularly inadequate for reproducing the physicality and warmth of human interactions in Brazil.[2] We must not discount the experiential significance and immediacy of local face-to-face relationships even as we acknowledge that telephones, e-mail, and other forms of interactive media are adding new dimensions to the local (Hannerz 1996b, 28).

Locality must be taken seriously not only because bodily experiences are indisputably powerful, but also because Japanese discourses on community still give great value to membership in local groups. The trappings of community that Japanese firms have offered (e.g. lifetime employment ideals, subsidized housing and meals, company trips, and year-end parties) have not always been completely satisfying, even for Japanese employees (see chapter 3). Nevertheless, such perks have represented an attractive ideal, the exclusion from which some Nikkeijin have felt keenly. Japanese discourse on the company constructed it as a community or family, and throughout the twentieth century women's dedication to the family and men's dedication to the firm were cast as patriotic contributions to Japan's race to modernize, industrialize, and catch up with the West (Nolte and Hastings 1991). Nikkeijin have had their most extensive contact with Japanese in the workplace. Consequently, the alienation that at least some Nikkeijin have felt in Japan has resulted from their exclusion from workplace communities.

At least among one group of transnational migrants, local communities were of great significance. The ongoing transnational connections with Brazil through newspapers, videos, letters, telephone calls, and trips played a large role in defining Japanese Brazilian migrants' sense of identity, and yet these influences often existed in conjunction with, rather than in exclusion of, identification with locally based contexts in Japan. Community was defined through interactions between Japanese and Nikkeijin, a process that sometimes ended in Nikkeijin exclusion and alienation. When Japanese workplaces failed the Nikkeijin by failing to fulfill the minimal criteria of

[1] I thank Debbora Battaglia for suggesting this adjective.
[2] See Linger (2001) for a discussion of Brazilian understandings of human warmth (*calor humano*).

[7]

community—a regularly interacting group of people who treated each other with respect and dignity—they turned not only toward transnational identifications with Brazil, but also toward local communities fashioned primarily by and for Nikkeijin themselves (see chapters 4 and 5).

Since the early 1990s, Nikkeijin have developed social networks that have made their lives in Japan more than an economic venture. Nikkeijin have found their lives within Brazilian ethnic enclaves in Japan sufficiently fulfilling to extend their stays through a long recession that has curtailed overtime work and reduced base wages. Some Nikkeijin transnationals have shuttled back and forth between Japan and Brazil. Some have returned permanently to Brazil. Others, however, have begun to settle in Japan, while maintaining their identification with things Brazilian. This book focuses primarily on this latter group and explores the structural factors and dynamic processes that have contributed to the formation of Nikkeijin as a distinct ethnic minority within Japan.

Mediating Institutions

Foreign workers in Japan have attracted the attention of many sociologists, economists, and political scientists. Several broad surveys have gauged the employment conditions and attitudes of foreign workers (Kitagawa 1993, Kokusai Kyōryoku Jigyōdan 1992). Other studies have focused more on the needs of Japanese businesses and the policies and social services of Japanese governmental and nongovernmental organizations (Miyajima and Kajita 1996, Tezuka 1995, Komai 1995, Shimada 1994, Ikegami 1997, Maniwa 1997). Anthropologists and sociologists conducting research with Japanese Brazilians have focused on ethnicity and identity (Tsuda 1996, Linger 2001, Yamanaka 2000, Shimizu 1997, Higuchi and Takahashi 1998a). Few scholars, however, have emphasized the connection of ethnicity and political-economic structures in relation to Nikkeijin. Ethnicity in industrial society cannot be fully understood without taking into account various types of work processes and labor markets (Bonacich and Modell 1980, di Leonardo 1984). In addition, the relationship between the construction of ethnic identity and both local and national government policies and ideologies demands consideration (see Anderson 1991, Espiritu 1992).

Some social scientists explain the tensions between Nikkeijin and Japanese in terms of cultural incompatibility (see Watanabe 1995). Although Japanese employers interpreted higher rates of job separation as indicative of Brazilian self-interest and irresponsibility, such behavioral patterns were not the result of cultural differences alone. They were related to the mar-

[8]

ginalization of Nikkeijin into positions that were explicitly meant to be temporary. An exclusive focus on cultural explanations fails to acknowledge structural reasons for Nikkeijin exclusion from workplace communities. A variety of factors have worked to exclude Nikkeijin from such communities.

Immigration policy also affected the discourse about and treatment of migrants in Japan. Immigration policy that gave preference to Nikkeijin over other foreigners saddled Asian workers with a stigma of illegality; Iranian, Pakistani, Bangladeshi, Filipino, Chinese, Korean, and other Asian migrants had overstayed their tourist visas and worked in Japan without formal documentation in small construction firms and manufacturing subcontractors (see Okuda and Tajima 1991, 1993).[3] Pressured by groups concerned with foreigners' impact on the social order, the Japanese government in 1989 stiffened penalties for employers of undocumented foreign workers; the penalties called for up to three years in jail and fines of up to two million yen (roughly $20,000). Migrant workers without regular visa status had little recourse if their employers charged exorbitant fees for transportation, meals and lodging, or failed to pay their full salaries or compensation in cases of workplace injury. The stigma and condition of illegality ironically forced a more complete assimilation among many Asian foreign workers to the norms of the Japanese workplace, in contrast to Nikkeijin, who, having formal legal status, were better able to resist such norms. They had greater flexibility to find different employment and could also sometimes engage the legal system, with the help of Japanese volunteers, to sue their employers when their rights were violated, potentially forcing their employers to accommodate a degree of difference.

At the same time, however, Nikkeijin were marginalized in relation to Japanese workers within the segmented labor market, a condition that affected all aspects of their relations with Japanese. In the U.S. context, Lamphere has written:

> "Mediating institutions" often act to contain and peripheralize newcomers, keeping them in marginal English-as-a-second-language classes, dead-end manufacturing and service jobs, and in separate apartment buildings within a complex. . . . The lack of integration between newcomers and established residents is the product of subtle micro-level structuring of the labor process at work, scheduling of classes and extracurricular programs at school, and landlords' policies in apartment complexes. (Lamphere 1992, 29)

[3] See also Ventura (1992) for an account of Filipino day laborers, and Nishiyama (1994) for an account of Iranians in Japan. See Komai (1995) and Lie (2001) for overviews of the debate over foreigners in the late 1980s and early 1990s; also see volumes on migrant workers in Japan edited by Hook and Weiner (1992), Weiner and Hanami (1998), and Douglass and Roberts (2000).

The labor market and immigration policy can be considered "mediating institutions" because of the way they have shaped interactions between Nikkeijin and Japanese. As chapters 3 and 4 illustrate, the segmented labor market marginalized Nikkeijin as contract workers in large firms and as brokered workers in smaller ones, statuses that effectively excluded them from membership in workplace communities. Although many Nikkeijin willingly accepted that they had been hired by employment brokers rather than directly by the manufacturing firms where they worked, others who desired more stable employment found this arrangement frustrating and alienating. Brokered workers were the first to be laid off and were denied access to health insurance and to other benefits permanent workers received.

Fieldwork Sites

The bulk of my fieldwork was conducted between 1994 and 1996 in Hamamatsu, an industrial city of 560,000 in Shizuoka Prefecture. Since the end of World War II, Hamamatsu's population has more than doubled, drawing rural Japanese migrants to work in its rapidly growing industrial sector. The population rose from 259,421 in 1947 to 443,352 in 1970. Thereafter it increased at a somewhat slower rate, reaching 562,702 in December 1994 (Hamamatsu-shi 1995a, 13–14). Of the total population of roughly 560,000 in 1991, 307,326 were employed, including 100,440 in the manufacturing sector (ibid., 30). While the manufacturing sector comprised 22.5 percent of all jobs in Japan as a whole, it comprised about 33 percent of jobs in Hamamatsu (Asahi Shimbun 1996, 97).

Lying in the heartland of the Japanese auto industry, Hamamatsu has spawned an impressive lineup of internationally recognized businesses. Suzuki, Yamaha, and Honda all started there, as did Kawai pianos and Roland, maker of electronic keyboards and synthesizers. Hamamatsu also had the largest number of Brazilian residents of any Japanese municipality. The booming economy of the late 1980s led to a more than 400 percent increase in the number of registered foreign residents, from 2,557 in 1988 to 11,456 in 1992 (Hamamatsu-shi 1995b, 29). Few of the long-term and permanent foreign residents in Hamamatsu were from Europe or North America. Nearly 70 percent were Nikkeijin from Brazil and Peru. Koreans, Chinese, Filipinos, and Vietnamese followed in rapidly descending order (Hamamatsu-shi 1995a). By 1997, the number of Brazilians alone surpassed 9,000. Including neighboring townships, Brazilians numbered about 20,000. Most of them worked for subcontractors that supplied parts to the larger manufacturers. In fact, 90 percent of foreigners in Hamamatsu worked in the manufacturing sector.[4] Of these, roughly 76 percent worked in the auto industry, the remainder in electronics and assorted other sectors (Hello Work 1995).

Several other industrial cities in Japan have attracted Nikkeijin migrants. Nagoya and Toyota in Aichi Prefecture (see Yamashita 2001, Linger 2001) and the town of Ōizumi and the city of Ōta in Gumma Prefecture (see Tsuda 1996) had large Brazilian populations. Many Nikkeijin in Japan were concentrated in a short string of highly industrialized prefectures running from Aichi through Shizuoka, Gumma, Nagano, and Kanagawa, to Tokyo. Others lived scattered in different regions from Hiroshima in the southwest, to Toyama on the Sea of Japan, up to Hokkaido in the north. I did research in Hamamatsu because of the high concentration of Nikkeijin and because its size, in relation to the much larger Nagoya or Tokyo, made it a more manageable research site. Nikkeijin were more visible in Hamamatsu and were the subject of much public discourse, yet their presence did not have as transformative an impact as it has had in smaller cities, such as Ōta or Ōizumi, where Nikkeijin composed as much as 10 percent of the population.

My fieldwork focused on two broad categories: workplaces (chapters 3 and 4) and residential neighborhoods (chapters 5 and 6). In these chapters, I explore the ways in which community was rhetorically and practically constituted. This is also the focus of chapter 2, which considers senses of belonging to national community. In this chapter, I examine various definitions of "Nikkeijin" with particular attention to how national and ethnic belonging was narrated during an annual conference sponsored by the Japanese Foreign Ministry and Federation of Prefectures. The official promotion of identification between Nikkeijin and Japanese may have played a part in the 1989 changes in immigration policy that facilitated visa applications for Nikkeijin.

In chapter 3, I focus on Japanese workers and their relations with foreign workers in a large automotive plant. Yusumi Motors (pseudonym), one of Hamamatsu's largest employers, has been able to offer its core permanent workers lifetime employment, seniority wages, and other benefits common among large firms in Japan and which have provided the basis for a community feel in the workplace (see Abegglen 1958, Dore 1973, Rohlen 1974). Some have suggested that the community model in Japanese firms would not be able to survive the corporate restructuring brought on by the Heisei era recession that began in the 1990s. My research indicates, however, that Japanese workers' sense of community within the Yusumi work-

---

[4] This figure is based on foreigners hired directly by manufacturing businesses and does not include the majority of foreign workers who were hired through employment brokers. Nevertheless, the figures suggest the concentration of foreign workers in the manufacturing sector overall.

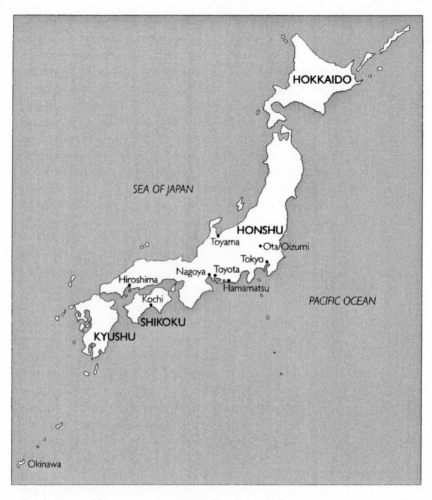

Map of Japan. Nikkeijin were concentrated in the central region of Japan, especially in the industrial belt from Nagoya to Tokyo.

place differed widely according to the success they had in competition with Japanese peers for limited promotion opportunities. The frustration of those who were unable to realize their career goals colored the way they perceived membership in their firm. It was in such a context that foreign workers made their entry and stimulated a discourse among Japanese workers and managers about the community of the Japanese workplace.

In chapter 4 I shift my focus toward the smaller subcontracting firms that hired the majority of Nikkeijin. Although this chapter also explores the ways in which workplace communities were defined, it focuses on the dynamic processes by which community was negotiated when relations among its members came under strain. The chapter specifically examines the interactions of workers and managers in the aftermath of workplace accidents. Although many observers assumed that Japanese cultural proclivities discouraged workers from confronting their firms in adversarial relationships, some were willing to do so when management failed to apologize or to offer other sincere expressions of remorse. As this chapter illustrates, apology and other respectful treatment by management could go a long way toward mending relationships with Nikkeijin as well as with Japanese workers. Managers often failed to extend such gestures, however, to workers (mostly Nikkeijin) who were hired through employment brokers, thus precipitating more dramatic ruptures of workplace communities.

Chapters 5 and 6 examine the ways in which communities were defined and membership negotiated in neighborhood settings. Chapter 5 traces the creation and eventual demise of a Brazilian culture center. The culture center was intended as a refuge from the materialism and competitive economic forces that determined so much of Nikkeijin migrants' lives in Japan. For two years, it provided those who felt excluded from social life at the workplace a meaningful alternative. Unfortunately, the leader was unable to sustain the idealism of the center in the face of his Japanese landlord's and Nikkeijin collaborators' economic interests. The center's short life was indicative of the ephemeral quality of the migrants' social landscape. Nevertheless, the feelings that motivated the culture center have continued to be fairly widespread among Nikkeijin in Japan. The center embodied a spirit of ethnic Brazilian community. Even as Nikkeijin learned Japanese and became accustomed to work and life in Japan, few began to see themselves as Japanese. On the contrary, the longer they stayed, the more they thought of themselves as a distinct Brazilian minority within Japan.

Although Japanese often criticized Nikkeijin unwillingness to live by Japanese rules in workplace and neighborhood contexts, certain occasions indicated that the Japanese might welcome Nikkeijin differences into their communities. The most dramatic example of this occurred during the annual Hamamatsu Kite Festival, which is the focus of chapter 6. In 1994 and

1995, I participated in monthlong preparations for the festival in a Japanese neighborhood organization dominated by shop owners and blue-collar workers. Members of this neighborhood prided themselves in belonging to one of the original founding neighborhoods of what has become the official festival of the entire city, and they look down on some of the newer middle-class neighborhoods that have recently joined the festival. In this chapter, I document and analyze how status conflicts between Japanese white-collar and blue-collar workers indirectly brought certain Japanese blue-collar workers closer to migrant workers. The members of one working-class neighborhood incorporated Brazilians and Brazilian music into the "traditional" Japanese festivities in a more meaningful way than that achieved by the much more widespread middle-class proponents of "internationalization" (*kokusaika*). Although academic literature on immigration often blames native blue-collar workers for tense relations with migrants, the cultural syncretism that was apparent during the kite festival reflected more complex relationships between class, nativism, and foreign workers.

Presentations and Perceptions of Self during Fieldwork

Within each context, my approach was colored by the conviction that anthropological research should be directed toward "assist[ing] society in solving social problems" (Greenwood et al. 1993, 176). Most of the contexts I entered involved a sometimes tense confrontation between at least two distinct groups, however, each of which had a quite different understanding of what problems needed solving. I was rarely in a position to act as mediator. In most cases, Japanese managers, bureaucrats, and neighborhood association leaders regarded me as a student. Nikkeijin did as well, although when I worked with the volunteer group Hamamatsu Overseas Laborers Solidarity, they saw me as an advocate—someone who helped foreign workers. My sympathetic portrayal of Nikkeijin in Hamamatsu in part grew out of the conditions in which they lived and worked, as well as what I considered to be distorted information that some Japanese bureaucrats and social scientists disseminated about foreign workers (see chapter 4).

I was not always a student in the eyes of my Nikkeijin and Japanese friends and acquaintances. I quickly developed an expanding circle of friends who enjoyed what they saw as my heroic efforts to gain fluency in Portuguese. I would go out with them to barbecues, discos, restaurants, and amusement parks, but I was initially limited to interviewing people who spoke either Japanese or English fairly well. By the end of my fieldwork, however, most Nikkeijin had enough confidence in my Portuguese that they did not resort to Japanese except when describing interactions or conversations they had had in Japanese. Many peppered their speech with creolized expressions of Japanese and Portuguese.

The fact that my mother is Japanese may have facilitated my relations with both Japanese and Japanese Brazilians. When Nikkeijin referred to me as a *descendente* (descendant of Japanese), they constructed a shared identity with me. They used others terms, such as "mestizo" (mixed Japanese and other ancestry) and "Americano," in both inclusive and exclusive ways. "Mestizo" simultaneously referred to my Japanese and non-Japanese ancestry, thus signifying both my identity and difference, except when used by someone else of mixed background, in which case it emphasized shared identity. "Americano" indicated that I shared the condition of being a foreigner in Japan at the same time it distinguished me from "Brasileiros." I tried to present myself to people using terms that emphasized a shared identity or experience. With Japanese Brazilians, I favored the term descendente. With Japanese I usually mentioned that my mother was Japanese. These shared identities may have sometimes helped establish relationships, but they never assured me of them. To a great extent, these terms of affiliation had to be earned over time through my actions. It was through reciprocating gifts, sending cards, or even just relishing Japanese food when dining together that some Japanese would note appreciatively that "after all, your mother is Japanese" (*yappari okāsan wa nihonjin*). With Japanese Brazilians, my increasingly successful effort to improve my Portuguese as well as my regular interactions over a long period proved more likely to assure my relationships with them.

Japanese friends and acquaintances referred to me as *Amerikajin* (American), *hāfu* ("half" Japanese), Nikkeijin, or *daigakuinsei* (graduate student), depending on the person and the context. As with the Brazilian terms of address, these could be used in inclusive or exclusive ways. Unlike Brazilians, for whom the anthropologist is a relatively familiar figure (even if most often associated with those who work among Amazonian tribes), few Japanese had any idea of what an anthropologist did. "Daigakuinsei" (graduate student) was a recognizable category that placed me within an academic environment but in a position of immaturity in relation to university professors, who were often accorded more respectful, but also more cautious, treatment. I could heighten my status if I so chose by specifying that I was completing a doctoral course (*hakase katei*).

At times I found that I had achieved more intimacy or informality in relationships than I was comfortable with. In addition to referring to me as "Americano," "mestizo," and "descendente," some Nikkeijin also called me *"antropólogo"* or *"antropólogo picareta"* (half-assed anthropologist)—the latter term applied by friends who did not understand how going with them to bowling lanes, discos, and barbecues constituted anthropological research. Although the term was said in jest, I did not appreciate it when one friend occasionally introduced me to strangers as a phony anthropologist. Also, the constant sexual jokes involving accusations of homosexuality and masturbation that certain male friends flung at each other and at me at times tried my patience. Some of them tested the limits of my identification with them when they joked about my Jewish heritage. On several occasions when out to eat with a group of five or six, one of them would suggest that I pay for everyone's meal. Any hesitation on my part elicited a mutter of *"Judeu"* followed by laughter and a closed fist indicating my unwillingness to part with money.

I would return their accusations of stinginess in kind, but their use of the Jewish stereotype hurt me and threatened the relationships that I had worked to develop. It was difficult at times to distance myself from the immediacy of these relationships and to think about how larger contexts may have influenced specific actions or postures.[5] When the first Nikkeijin started migrating to Japan in the late 1980s, their primary goal was to save as much money in as little time as possible in Japan and take it back to buy a house or to start a business in Brazil. In later years, migrants thought more about how to enjoy their time in Japan and became conspicuous consumers. Nikkeijin in Japan made enough to travel both within Japan and to other parts of Asia. They purchased cars, expensive clothes, computers, and a host of other electronic appliances on the wages they made in factories. Some Japanese managers said that Nikkeijin had been hardworking early on but later became less motivated, and connected it to their changed attitudes toward savings and consumption in Japan (see chapter 5). Many Nikkeijin, on the other hand, evaluated the newfound attitudes in a more positive light and defended their right to live life fully in Japan instead of working three hours of overtime six days per week. Viewed from such a perspective, I could understand my acquaintances' jabs at stinginess, although I was still unhappy about their use of the Jewish stereotype.

Many Nikkeijin were professional workers for much of their careers in Brazil. By taking blue-collar jobs in Japan, they were able to make much more than they had in Brazil, especially given the inflation of the late 1980s, but many felt this shift as a serious drop in status. Some complained strongly about the treatment they encountered in Japanese workplaces, being ordered about roughly and shouted at when they misunderstood instructions. These kinds of interactions may have been especially difficult for

---

[5] See José Limón's analysis of jokes and dances among Mexican American men as expressions of virtuoso masculinity (1994, chapters 6 and 7). Limón suggests that the jokes and dances provide a way for these working-class men to create value within racial, ethnic, and socioeconomic circumstances that marginalize and stigmatize them.

someone who had been accustomed to a degree of respect defined in white-collar Brazilian terms. In their search for value and meaning in their lives in Japan, Nikkeijin often had no choice but to turn away from the workplace. Many found alternative sources of value in conspicuous consumption, others in performances of masculinity, some in religious practice, many in celebrations of their Brazilian identities.

When I started my fieldwork in Hamamatsu, I made my status as an anthropologist clear to most people with whom I interacted. At times, however, there were some constraints on my ability to communicate my status. Managers at the factory I describe in chapter 3 agreed to give me access to the factory to conduct research on the condition that I worked on the assembly line like anyone else on a short-term contract. They did not want me to float around the factory, conducting interviews and hindering work. Throughout my stint in the factory, I grappled with the dilemma of how to present myself to my fellow workers. The managers had told only those in my work section and neighboring ones about me, but I made a point of informing those with whom I had more than casual interaction. But since I maintained the same work routine and wore the same uniform as everyone else, my status as an anthropologist was effectively camouflaged from many of the more than two thousand workers in the factory. Any context that is hierarchically organized and to which access is granted by those at the upper levels without the consultation of all other members of the group poses ethical dilemmas for researchers. Under those circumstances, I felt constrained and pulled by multiple obligations. I was responsible for working according to the terms of the agreement made during my job interview. I also felt a responsibility toward the people I worked and lived with, who had no say in granting me entry into their spaces, to be as nonintrusive as possible.

Everyone in the Brazilian culture center I describe in chapter 5 knew me as an anthropologist. Once again, however, my prolonged participation in the routines of the center allowed me to develop a degree of intimacy with many of its members that at times may have blurred my status. I was sympathetic to the ideals of the center. I helped raise money for it and publicized it among both my Japanese and Nikkeijin acquaintances. No one at the center foresaw the internal struggles that developed and eventually led to its demise, nor did I intend for the chapter to become a document of this turn of events. I hope that despite my occasional criticism of people at the center, my portrayal conveys a sense of their ideals and enthusiasm.

In writing this ethnography, I have necessarily highlighted certain events and issues while glossing over others. Some Nikkeijin may indeed have realized their expectations of self-understanding in Japan by adopting Japanese customs and by interacting and identifying primarily with Japanese as op-

[17]

posed to Brazilians. Some have moved back and forth between Brazil and Japan, while others have moved back more permanently to Brazil. A substantial number, however, have come to identify more strongly with things Brazilian even as they have started to settle permanently in Japan, and it is the process by which this has occurred that I explore most deeply. Before traveling to Japan, many older Nikkeijin—and some younger ones as well—conceived of themselves as both Brazilian and members of a Japanese diaspora in Brazil. Many had immersed themselves in Japanese music (Hosokawa 1995), cinema (Hosokawa 1999), and other cultural activities, looking with nostalgia *(kyōshū)* toward Japan as their ancestral homeland. From that perspective, their travel to Japan was a return to their ancestral homeland. However, after several years of working and living in Japan, many younger migrants developed their taste for Brazilian music and culture, looking back toward Brazil with yearning *(saudade)*, and in some respects conceived of themselves as members of a Brazilian diaspora and as an ethnic minority within Japan. In order to understand how this shift occurred, we must examine how Nikkeijin and Japanese have defined community and negotiated membership within local contexts, which were in part already structured by political and economic policies and institutions.

[2]

Transnational Identifications at the Conference for Overseas Japanese

Suzuki Shunichi, the head of the quasi-governmental Association for Overseas Japanese *(Kaigai Nikkeijin Kyōkai)* addressed a gathering of Japanese government and Nikkeijin representatives in 1990 with the following statement: "Through their industrious *(kimben)* and persevering *(nintai)* character, all Nikkeijin have earned the confidence [of those around them], and have created a firm standing for themselves in the political, economic, social, and cultural arenas of those countries [wherein they reside]" *(Kaigai Nikkeijin* no. 29, 39).[1] As is often the case in official ceremonies involving the Japanese government and Nikkeijin, participants rarely passed up opportunities to laud the character of Nikkeijin and the success that years of hard work overseas has brought.

In an amusement park outside Nagoya, waiting on an interminably long, snaking line for the biggest wooden roller coaster in Japan, Edivaldo Kishimoto joked about the predicament of most Brazilians working in Japan: "I'm a good worker; it's just that any idiot could do my job." He and I were at the park, enjoying a Saturday afternoon along with thousands of young Japanese and a surprising number of young Brazilians. In 1993, Edivaldo

---

[1] Japan's prefectural governments jointly chartered the Association for Overseas Japanese *(Kaigai Nikkeijin Kyōkai)*, which is also closely affiliated with the Ministry of Foreign Affairs *(gaimushō)*. Retired Foreign Ministry bureaucrats and prefectural directors have figured prominently in its administration. The annual Conference for Overseas Japanese *(Kaigai Nikkeijin Taikai)* is organized by the Association for Overseas Japanese and is sponsored by the Ministry of Foreign Affairs, the Japanese International Cooperation Association (JICA) *(Nihon Kokusai Kyōryoku Jigyōdan)*, and the Japan Foundation *(Nihon Kokusai Kōryū Kikin)*. JICA and the Japan Foundation also are affiliated with the Ministry of Foreign Affairs.

had been laid off his job as a geologist in a large Brazilian petrochemical firm. Soon thereafter, he moved to Japan, where he found work operating a metal stamping press for an auto parts maker. Thousands of times a day, he placed a section of sheet metal on the press, quickly moved his arms out of harm's way, and hit the button that brought the upper stamping block down with forty tons of force.

Suzuki Shunichi delivered his comments at a formal public event; Edivaldo Kishimoto made his in passing to a friend in an informal setting. Although the contexts were very different, the quotes reveal a gap between the ideologies promoted by government representatives and the experiences of Nikkeijin who have migrated to Japan. In terms of the everyday realities of the majority of Japanese Brazilians living and working in Japan, the rhetoric of the Conference for Overseas Japanese appeared somewhat spurious, yet over the years the conference has provided a forum that has helped maintain the connections between overseas communities and the Japanese government. In this context, both Japanese and Nikkeijin have constructed a shared identity drawing on the idiom of work and kinship, rituals of respect, and narratives of suffering and overcoming.

Edivaldo's remark constitutes a critique of such appeals to a shared identity, especially an identity based on attitudes toward work. He expressed the frustration that many educated Nikkeijin have felt working in Japan. Where was he headed? How did his life in Japan relate to the life he had been living in Brazil? What use was a special relationship with Japan if it only led to work opportunities that were demeaning? Edivaldo's repudiation of a strong identification with Japan was based on several years of working in Japanese factories. Before considering Nikkeijin experiences in Japan and their gradually increasing alienation from Japan, however, it is important to understand the nature of their past identification.

Japanese Diasporas

Several hundred Japanese went to work on Hawaii, on Guam, and in California in 1868 (Chan 1991, 11). They were among the earliest group of Japanese workers allowed to leave the country after the long period of official seclusion (1638–1853). The terrible conditions that were reported led to a halt of emigration, but by 1885 the Japanese government had started to actively promote emigration, a policy that continued until the early 1960s (Wakatsuki and Suzuki 1975). Over the decades, the destinations of Japanese migrants shifted through various parts of the Americas and Asia. Table 2.1 shows where and when Japanese settled abroad. Many more immigrated to Taiwan and Korea under Japanese colonial rule. In 1944 there

Table 2.1. Japanese Immigrants to Various Destinations in Prewar and Wartime Periods

	North America and Hawaii	Central and South America	Southeast Asia	Manchuria
1868–1898	89,962	0	0	0
1899–1924	302,772	70,588	37,060	0
1925–1931	14,417	82,885	25,376	0
1932–1941	4,258	91,063	25,740	180,534
1942–1943	0	0	0	89,473

Source: Tanaka 1991, 189.

were 397,090 Japanese residing in Taiwan and 712,583 in Korea (Tanaka 1991, 193). Almost all of those who had settled in these two colonies and Manchuria were repatriated at the end of the war. Most Japanese settlers in other regions remained where they were.

A small number of Japanese unofficially entered Brazilian Amazonia from Peru to work as rubber tappers in the first years of the twentieth century, but 1908 marks the official start of Japanese migration to Brazil. On June 18, 1908, a shipload of 781 Japanese migrants sailed into the port of Santos aboard the *Kasato-maru*.[2] The Brazilian government had been searching for alternative sources of labor for its vast coffee plantations. After slavery was abolished in 1888, the government encouraged immigrants from Europe to help settle the temperate southern states of Brazil— Rio Grande do Sul, Santa Catarina, Paraná, and São Paulo. Migrants came in the thousands, from Italy, Spain, Portugal, Germany, Poland, Lebanon, Syria, and Turkey, and other countries.

Brazilian leaders at the time were concerned about the assimilability of Asian immigrants and barred their entry through most of the 19th century (Lesser 1999, chapters 2 and 4). Unrest among European plantation workers and the growth of organized labor eventually persuaded the government to overcome reservations about Japanese racial differences, especially after hearing about the productivity of Japanese workers on Hawaiian plantations. In order to ensure a more docile workforce, Japanese immigrants were required to come in family units of at least three people. This policy resulted in a more even gender balance among Japanese migrants to Brazil than to other countries. For at least one generation, the rate of intermar-

---

[2] See Tomoo Handa (1980) for a detailed account of the earliest wave of migrants to the coffee plantations. See also Burajiru Nihon Imin Hachijūnen Shi Hensan I'inkai (1991). See Smith (1979) for a concise overview in English, and Smith et al. (1967) for an extensive annotated bibliography of earlier work in this area.

riage among Japanese migrants to Brazil was much lower than it was among Japanese who went to Peru.

Most early Japanese migrants to Brazil thought of themselves as sojourners with the dream of striking it rich *(ikkaku senkin)* and one day returning gloriously to Japan clad in finery *(nishiki'i kikoku)* (Maeyama 1996c, 177). This orientation toward Japan fluctuated depending on political and economic conditions in Japan and Brazil at different historical junctures. The history of Japanese migration to Brazil was not one of gradual and continuous assimilation into Brazil society.

In the 1920s, conditions allowed for complex affiliations, neither completely Japanese nor Brazilian. Anthropologist Maeyama Takashi suggests replacing the academic concept of gradual acculturation with Japanese Brazilians' own terminology (Maeyama 1996c). Some writers in the 1920s used the term *"wakon hakusai"* (Japanese spirit and Brazilian learning) to advocate the incorporation and adaptation of Brazilian qualities into the Japanese spirit. This term derived in part from the discourse on Japanese spirit and Western learning *(wakon yōsai)* of the Meiji period in Japan (1868–1912), when the Japanese government actively supported the introduction of Western European political, economic, bureaucratic, and industrial organization and technology.

In the latter 1930s, however, the Vargas government's assimilationist policies forced the closure of Japanese language schools and newspapers throughout Brazil. Along with the start of the Pacific war and spread of Japanese ultranationalist propaganda, a backlash arose among Japanese propagandists in Brazil who increasingly advocated *wakon wasai* (Japanese spirit and Japanese learning) in place of wakon hakusai (Maeyama 1996c, 186–88). The restrictions placed on the Japanese community, the spread of nationalist ideology, and the lack of Japanese language media coverage created conditions that fostered a millenarian movement among the Japanese migrants and their children. Many within the Japanese community supported the ultranationalist *kachi-gumi*, which refused to acknowledge Japan's defeat until several years after World War II. Members of this group cowed skeptics into silence by murdering numerous leaders of the realist *make-gumi* (see Maeyama 1982).[3]

At different points before and after the war, however, many first-generation migrants developed a strong sense of themselves as distinct from Japanese in Japan even while continuing to value their ties with Japan. Raising families and becoming accustomed to life in Brazil, Japanese migrants decided to settle there permanently. They no longer thought of themselves

---

[3] Karen Yamashita provides a vivid fictionalized account of these events in her novel *Brazil Maru* (1992).

negatively as Japanese displaced to Brazil, but positively as the parents and ancestors of Brazilians. Even some who had been Japanese ultranationalists in the 1940s became ardent patriots of Brazil (Maeyama 1996b, 238–40, Maeyama 1972).

They embraced a Brazilian identity while continuing to participate in Nikkeijin community associations and cooperatives. Many tried to teach their children and grandchildren Japanese and maintained a strong identification with things Japanese through such activities as sports and music. Some encouraged their children to study in Japan. In the United States, the history of internment during World War II motivated Japanese Americans to draw a sharp distinction between themselves and Japanese in Japan, a legacy that continues to distinguish Japanese American from Japanese Brazilian understandings of their relationship with Japan. In Brazil, Nikkeijin have developed a sense of themselves as Brazilians, but this has not come at the expense of their sense of continuity with their Japanese heritage. It is not uncommon for Japanese Brazilians to refer to themselves, and to be referred to by others, as "Nikkei," "nisei," or just plain "Japonês."[4]

Defining "Nikkeijin"

The term "Nikkeijin" itself reflects how Japanese conceive of their relationship to those who have migrated overseas and their descendants. "Nikkeijin" is composed of the Chinese characters that mean "sun line people," the "sun" referring to the first character of the term for Japan, *nihon*, which means "the origin of the sun." The imperial household traces its ancestry to the sun goddess Amaterasu of Japanese mythology. The term "Nikkeijin," however, does not normally refer to ethnically Japanese people residing in Japan, who are referred to as "Nihonjin" (or "Nipponjin"). "Nikkeijin" is a category without reference to a specific place. Although a literal reading of the term would include Japanese, "Nikkeijin" normally refers to those we may think of as "overseas Japanese," members of the Japanese diaspora. The term does not include Japanese students, tourists, or businesspeople working, traveling, or studying temporarily outside Japan.

The term "Nikkeijin" is used often in conjunction with terms of national affiliation. Thus, Japanese Americans are referred to as *Nikkei Amerikajin*, Japanese Brazilians as *Nikkei Burajirujin*, and Japanese Peruvians as *Nikkei*

---

[4] See Lesser (1999) for a discussion of what he refers to as the "hidden hyphen" in Brazilian ethnic terminology. According to Lesser, the usage of the unmodified "Japonês" in Brazil did not imply Nikkeijin exclusion from membership within the Brazilian nation. The assumption, rather, that Nikkeijin were members, made explicit hyphenated terminology superfluous.

Perujin. Other terms make distinctions among those who fall into the category of Nikkeijin. *Ijūsha* refers to Japanese who have settled in other countries. The generationally specific term *issei* (first generation) also refers to such immigrants. They are the first generation in their families to live overseas. *Nisei* (second generation) refers to the children who are born overseas. *Sansei* (third generation) refers to the grandchildren of the initial migrants.

Maeyama Takashi provides a useful table (Table 2.2) of the different ways in which Japanese, Japanese Brazilians, and Brazilians without Japanese ancestry have referred to themselves and to each other. The only places the term Nikkeijin appears in this table are in the margins as categories that Maeyama himself uses, and in the box that lists the terms that "Japanese migrants to Brazil" used to refer to "Nikkeijin born in Brazil." According to this table, the issei (first generation) did not use the term Nikkeijin in reference to themselves, but exclusively for their children and grandchildren born in Brazil. By choosing to name the middle category "Nikkeijin born in Brazil" rather than an unmodified "Nikkeijin," Maeyama leaves open the possibility the term Nikkeijin could apply to the first-generation migrants. Indeed, throughout many of the works in his 1996 collection of essays see 1996a), Maeyama uses the term Nikkeijin in this more inclusive sense.

Similarly, Fuchigami Eiji defines "Nikkeijin" broadly to refer to members of a migrant society *(ijūshakai no kōsei'in),* including the first-generation migrants themselves. He notes in the introduction to his book, however, that he generally uses this term to refer just to the second, third, and later generations of descendants to distinguish from the first generation. Furthermore, he makes a convention of writing the names of those born overseas in the phonetic syllabary known as katakana, a script often used to spell out foreign words that have entered the Japanese language. He writes the names of those who were born in Japan with the standard Chinese characters known as kanji. In doing so, Fuchigami recognizes that later genera-

Table 2.2. Relative Terms of Reference

Categorized	Speaker: Japanese migrants to Brazil (born in Japan)	Speaker: Nikkeijin born in Brazil	Speaker: Non-nikkei Brazilians
Japanese migrants to Brazil (born in Japan)	Nipponjin, issei	Japonês, issei	Japonês
Nikkeijin born in Brazil	nisei, sansei, yonsei Nikkeijin	nisei, Nihonjin, Brasileiro	Japonês
Non-nikkei Brazilians	gaijin, Burajirujin	gaijin, Brasileiro, etc.	Brasileiro, etc.

Source: Maeyama 1996b, 238.

tions of overseas Japanese rarely used Chinese characters to write their names, but his use of katakana for overseas Japanese names makes a distinction between them and the first-generation migrants (Fuchigami 1995, 3–4).[5]

The inclusive meaning of "Nikkeijin" has appeared in other contexts besides the writings of authors and academics such as Fuchigami and Maeyama. At the Conference for Overseas Japanese, "Nikkeijin" had a broad meaning that referred to both the first-generation migrants and their foreign-born descendants. The term "Nikkeijin" distinguished people of Japanese descent who were either born or residing permanently overseas from those who were born in Japan and who continued to live there. However, the term simultaneously referenced the connection between those living overseas and those living in Japan in its emphasis on genealogy— "people of the sun line." In this vision, all who descended from a common Japanese origin were linked in a fundamental way. Perhaps this is one reason the imperial family, popularly considered the most ancient of Japanese families from which all others branched, holds such an important place among those Nikkeijin who identify with Japan.

Japanese immigration policy has produced other definitions of "Nikkeijin." The majority of first-generation Japanese migrants to Brazil who still held their Japanese citizenship faced no legal or bureaucratic hurdles to travel and work in Japan. From the perspective of the Japanese government, issei were Japanese. The same was true for a minority of second- or third-generation Japanese Brazilians who held dual citizenship. Having been born in Brazil, nisei and sansei automatically had Brazilian citizenship, and if their parents registered them with a Japanese consulate within thirty days of birth they could have Japanese citizenship too. Most first-generation parents, however, did not do this for their children, so the majority of second- and third-generation Nikkeijin had to obtain visas to travel to Japan.

Starting in 1989, the Japanese immigration bureau expedited the processing of visa applications from second- and third-generation Nikkeijin. They were issued two types of visa—the "spouse or child of Japanese national" *(nihonjin no haigūsha nado)* visa and the "long-term" *(teijūsha)* visa—for periods of between six months and three years. These visas carried no restrictions on the work they could perform in Japan. The immigration bureau generally gave second-generation (nisei) applicants visas for

---

[5] In Takahashi Hidemine's book, *Nise nipponjin tambōki* (1995), the author refers to Japanese Peruvians and other Nikkeijin by writing the term "Nipponjin" in katakana. Both Takahashi and Fuchigami use katakana to indicate that which is more foreign. See Marilyn Ivy's article in *Public Culture* 1, no. 1 (fall 1988) for a discussion of the use of the katakana script in Japanese travel advertising to evoke not just the foreign but also the temporally distant or culturally exotic within Japan itself. Authors take certain liberties with terms that do not reflect spoken usage.

three years, and third-generation (sansei) applicants visas for just one year. Fourth and later generations were required to go through a much more complicated and time-consuming application process, which required a family member with residence in Japan to guarantee their status (Sellek 1997, 202).[6]

Japanese immigration policy implied that the "Japanese-ness" of Nikkeijin diminished with each generation. At the Conference for Overseas Japanese in 1994, Japanese Brazilian representatives criticized the Japanese Immigration Bureau practice of granting second-generation Nikkeijin longer visas than third-generation Nikkeijin. In fact, the term "nisei," which signifies second generation in Japanese, is often used by Nikkeijin in Brazil to refer to all generations of Japanese Brazilians born in Brazil (see Table 2.2).

As a foreign researcher, I was initially issued a cultural activities *(bunka katsudō)* visa when I went to Japan. In order to conduct participant observation in the factories where Nikkeijin were working, however, I found it advantageous to change my visa status to that which other Nikkeijin had received. As a second-generation Nikkeijin, I had to supply a birth certificate and an official copy of the family registry *(koseki tōhon)* of one parent, in my case my mother, from the town or city hall where she was from. Immigration officials verified Japanese ancestry by matching the parent's name on the applicant's birth certificate and the name in the family registry. The immigration bureau took between two weeks and several months to process these visa applications. A third-generation Nikkeijin had to supply a birth certificate, the birth certificate of one parent, and the family registry of the same parent. Often immigration officials also requested to see marriage certificates for parents and grandparents. In the case of Peruvians, minor discrepancies in the way Japanese names were transliterated on different documents by Peruvian officials unfamiliar with Japanese names led Japanese officials to reject applications (Fuchigami 1995, 49–54).

The suspicions that Japanese officials had of Nikkeijin from Peru were heightened in late 1992, when Japanese newspapers published several stories about Peruvians without Japanese ancestry who had bought or forged documents necessary to apply for visas as Japanese Peruvians.[7] In a sense,

---

[6] In the mid-1990s, there were still relatively few fourth-generation Japanese Brazilians of adult age. Some third-generation Japanese Brazilians live in Japan with their fourth-generation children. As of now, their children are not eligible to work even when they reach 15, which is the legal minimum age at which one can work in Japan unless special visas are issued to them.

[7] An article in the May 15, 1992 edition of the *Asahi Shimbun*, the daily newspaper with the largest circulation in Japan, reported that certain documents necessary for proving Japanese ancestry had been forged and sold to as many as five thousand Peruvians in the year and a half after revision of the immigration law in 1990. On Dec 26, 1991, the same newspaper reported that organized-crime syndicates may have been involved in obtaining the Japanese family registries of Japanese Peruvians which could be sold for up to $3,000. Evidence for the black market in docu-

[26]

approval of visa applications became the Japanese government's official validation of Nikkeijin identity.

Residency and ancestry formed two crucial elements in the dominant definition of who was Japanese. Some Japanese saw Nikkeijin as an attractive alternative to other kinds of foreign labor because of their shared ancestry. However, connections between Nikkeijin and Japanese were social and historical, not natural, and as such had to be actively maintained to survive. At the annual Conference for Overseas Japanese, overseas participants diminished distinctions between first-generation Japanese immigrants and their children while emphasizing common ties to their ancestral homeland. Japanese government officials and Nikkeijin participants emphasized common ancestry through the use of the idiom of family. Common ancestry was also linked to shared cultural characteristics that overcame the different geographical contexts of Japanese and Nikkeijin experience and unified them through isomorphic historical narratives.

The Conference for Overseas Japanese

The first Conference for Overseas Japanese took place in Tokyo on May 2–4, 1957. It had a different name at the time—Conference in Commemoration of Japan's Induction into the United Nations, and the Reunion of Overseas Japanese." The idea for the conference came after a visit that several diet (parliament) members made to Japanese American communities in the United States. The stories Nikkeijin told them of the economic and psychological hardships of internment motivated these diet members to hold an event for Nikkeijin "in the spirit of consolation for their long suffering (nagai kurō)." (*Kaigai Nikkeijin* no. 6, 13).

The participants in the first conference included many political and business leaders of the day. In attendance were Prime Minister Kishi Shinsuke, Finance Minister (later Prime Minister) Ikeda Hayato, Transportation Min-

---

ments was found in the classified ads of a Lima daily newspaper. On Nov 29, 1991, the *Mainichi Shimbun*, another Japanese daily, ran a full-page story complete with photo of the incriminating page from the Peruvian newspaper. Certain Japanese Peruvians had advertised the sale of official copies of their family registries (*koseki tōhon*), the key document from the Japanese side necessary to establish Japanese ancestry. When a Peruvian bought an official copy of a family registry, he or she would have all the birth and marriage certificates made to correspond. In many cases, corrupt bureaucrats in charge of such certificates in Peruvian city governments made the bogus documents for a hefty fee (Fuchigami 1995, 25). As a result of these revelations, it became very difficult for many Peruvians, including those with Japanese ancestry, to renew or obtain visas after October 1992. Hundreds have been denied. According to the director of a labor union for Peruvian workers, these stories have had material consequences, with Peruvian wages dropping to 70 percent of that of Brazilians' (*Asahi Shimbun*, Oct. 11, 1992).

ister Miyazawa Taneo, Agriculture Minister Ide Ichitaro, Commerce Minister Mizuta Mikio, Tokyo Governor Yasui Sei'ichiro, Japan Newspaper Association President Murayama Nagayo, Tokyo Chamber of Commerce director Fujiyama Ai'ichiro (also president of Dai Nihon Seito sugar company), and several members of the diet (ibid., 14). During the ceremonies, Prime Minister Kishi saluted overseas Japanese communities for lending support to Japan in the early postwar years, when so many Japanese were close to starvation:

> During the extremely difficult period right after the war, all of our overseas brothers *(kaigai dōhō)* held out a warm hand in the support of us of the motherland *(bokoku)*. We cannot thank them enough for the comfort and encouragement they provided, and I would like to take this opportunity to once again express our deep gratitude (ibid., 15).

The story of these relief efforts for Japan was resurrected in the 1995 conference commemorating the fiftieth anniversary of the war's end. In the previously quoted passage, Prime Minister Kishi naturalized the relationship between Japanese in Japan and Japanese overseas by referring to overseas Japanese as "kaigai dōhō" ("overseas of the same womb"). He also referred to Japan as "bokoku," which could be translated as "mother country." Thus the metaphors in Kishi's address suggested that Nikkeijin and Japanese both came from the womb of mother Japan. The term "dōhō" is still used by some elderly representatives of overseas Japanese communities, not just to celebrate connections, but also to criticize neglect of relations while campaigning for greater support from the Japanese government.

The second conference was held three years later, in 1960. The third was held in 1962, and thereafter it became an annual affair. The ceremonial aspects of the conference quickly became routinized, with the addition of the now climactic greetings from members of the imperial family starting with the sixth conference in 1965. Over the years, however, the attendance of Japanese political and economic leaders has dropped, reflecting the decline in importance and status of the overseas communities in Japanese eyes. Although emigration in the postwar period had never reached significant levels (reaching a peak of about 16,000 in 1959), the flow of Japanese abroad had declined to a trickle by the mid-1960s. During that time, rapid growth of the Japanese economy created an abundance of jobs in Japanese urban centers that redirected migration from international to domestic circuits.

I attended the Conference for Overseas Japanese in 1994 and 1995. The overall schedule of events at the conference was much the same both years. The first day was devoted to discussions between representatives from the overseas communities and officials from the Ministry of Foreign Affairs and

Japan International Cooperation Association (JICA). Based on these discussions, the overseas representatives drafted a formal list of requests to the Japanese government which they presented the following day. They asked for cooperation in resolving various issues faced by overseas communities such as welfare support for the aged and Japanese language instruction for younger generations. They requested that the Japanese government consider establishing an absentee ballot system so Japanese nationals overseas could participate in Japanese elections.[8] They wanted more assistance for various cultural exchange programs. They asked the Japanese people to open their hearts to Nikkeijin migrants so that they would recognize Japan as their motherland. They stressed that overseas communities were undergoing a difficult transformation because so many young adults had departed for jobs in Japan, and asked for the Japanese government's support and understanding during this transition.

Of the 437 people who attended the conference in 1994, 150 were either from the Japanese government or related organizations and companies, and 287 were Nikkeijin. Of these, 79 were prefectural scholarship students starting a period of study in Japanese universities, and 25 were representatives of the various overseas communities. Many of the remaining 183 indicated that they had personal or business matters to attend to in Japan in addition to the conference. Those who attended were members of the Nikkeijin elite—leaders of overseas community organizations, scholarship students, business leaders, and those who were simply wealthy enough to afford the airfare and lodging even when the exchange rate was so unfavorable for foreigners traveling to Japan (the rate hovered just above 100 yen to the U.S. dollar).

The second day involved speeches in the morning capped by the highlight of the conference, appearances by members of the imperial family. Many Japanese journalists gathered in the main hall and set up their equipment to cover that year's imperial representatives, Crown Prince Naruhito and Princess Masako. The journalists lined the length of one wall with cameras sporting powerful telephoto lenses mounted on tripods, and waited patiently through the long series of speeches and greetings by lesser officials. When the speeches finally ended shortly before lunchtime, someone started playing softly on an organ near the stage. A plainclothes officer sat down next to me and asked where I was from. I had an aisle seat, which put me within arm's reach of the imperial couple as they approached the stage, and he was apparently checking all suspect-looking characters.

For security reasons, the crowd was asked to remain seated for the entrance of the crown prince and Masako. In their excitement, however, many in the audience rose to their feet and applauded when they caught sight of

---

[8] An absentee ballot system was instituted in 2000 (see Roth forthcoming).

the imperial couple. Cameras flashed and the organ music reached a crescendo as the two made their way along the aisle to the front. Once they were seated on stage, an official made a short introduction and gave the floor to the crown prince. His greeting lasted no longer than two or three minutes. He mentioned the important role that the conference had played since its inception as a bridge connecting Japan and the countries in which Nikkeijin resided, and the contribution that Nikkeijin had made to the development of those countries, to cultural exchange and understanding. Finally, he prayed for the success of the conference, for the meaningful resolution of any issues Nikkeijin representatives had raised the previous day during their discussions with government officials, and for their safe return to their various countries after enjoying a beautiful May in Japan.

After the prince's speech came a presentation of flowers to Princess Masako. One at a time, a woman from each of the countries represented at the conference walked the length of the room, carrying a long-stemmed rose. At the foot of the stage a vase had been set up in which they placed the roses. Then they turned to Princess Masako and said a few words of greeting, often pointing out the similarities between the flowers and scenery of their own countries and those of Japan, and inviting the imperial couple to visit. The Mexican representative pointed out that the jacaranda blooms at the same time as the cherry blossom in Japan. The Philippine representative invited the prince and princess to her hometown of Baguio, comparing it to the scenic Japanese mountain resort town of Karuizawa, where the royals had a retreat. When the last Nikkeijin representative had inserted her rose, she offered the vase of roses to Masako, who graciously accepted, and the ceremony came to a close. With Nikkeijin representatives from each country paying tribute to the imperial family, the ceremony could have been interpreted as a representation of a former empire.[9]

The women representing the various countries in this ceremony were of various generations, each with its own style of presentation. Older women made their remarks with great reverence and emotion; younger ones seemed nervous at having to stand in front of so many people and to speak in a language in which they were not fluent. Even a native speaker would have had to practice the honorific and humble forms necessary for the occasion.

The next year, the emperor's brother Prince Hitachinomiya and his wife, Princess Hanako, presided over the flower ceremony. I attended with the maternal aunt of Edivaldo, my Brazilian friend from Hamamatsu. This aunt, who was sixty-three years old, had been born in Japan and moved to Brazil with her family at the age of three. Even after all those years, however, her Japanese, both spoken and written, was better than her Por-

[9] I thank Stefan Senders for suggesting this interpretation.

tuguese. This was her first trip back to Japan; she had visited the town in Kōchi Prefecture where she had been born and had visited her Brazilian-born sisters who were working in Osaka and Hamamatsu with their families. At the end of the flower presentation, as the prince and princess made their way down the aisle toward us and the exit, my companion raised her hand tentatively and waved to the royal couple. Her eyes filled with tears; her expression was both timid and joyful. Clearly, this was one of the high points of her nostalgic trip back to Japan and achieved the kind of bonding that the conference organizers had intended.

The final day was dedicated to a tour of Tokyo which highlighted the imperial castle grounds, diet building, the Yasukuni Shrine (the controversial shrine to Japan's war dead), and the Tokyo Metropolitan Government Office building. A final evening dinner party was held at the prestigious banquet hall Chinzanso, on the grounds of the former Tokyo residence of Yamagata Aritomo, founder of Japan's modern military.

Nikkeijin were not the only marginal group in recent Japanese history whose representatives have been received by Japanese officials in the capital and guided on a tour of the imperial institution and other government sites. In 1937, on the occasion of the Japanese diet's revision of the Ex-Aborigine Protection Law designed to speed Ainu assimilation into Japanese society, Ainu leaders were brought to Tokyo to observe the passage of the bill, after which they were taken on a pilgrimage to the Imperial Palace, the Shinjuku Gyoen (Shinjuku Imperial Gardens) and the Meiji and Ise Shrines. From the perspective of Japanese political leaders in the 1930s, these rituals marked the completion of the processes of civilizing and Japanizing the Ainu (Takagi 1993).[10] At the center of the assimilation process was the inculcation of an attitude of reverence and worship toward the emperor. In the case of Nikkeijin in Latin America, the appearance of the imperial family at the conference, along with the tour of the imperial and national sites, has served as a means of maintaining their bonds to Japan.

The Narrative of Suffering and Overcoming

Identification with Japan was encouraged at the conference not only through visits to imperial and government sites and through the idiom of family that bound Nikkeijin to Japanese as overseas siblings but also through what I call the narrative of suffering and overcoming—a narrative of Nikkeijin and Japanese postwar history. Both Nikkeijin and Japanese

---

[10] See also Fujitani (1996) on the significance of imperial sites in inculcating nationalism among a much wider Japanese population during the Meiji, Taishō, and Shōwa eras.

I brought two Nikkeijin friends from Hamamatsu to the newly built Tokyo metropolitan government building in the fall of 1995.

drew on this narrative to express their defining characteristics, and it functioned as proof of their shared identity. Here is what Prime Minister Nakasone had to say at the 1983 conference:

> Overseas Nikkeijin, up until this very day, are in the process of overcoming numerous bitter hardships and ordeals (*ikuta no konnan to shiren*), and have earned deep trust and friendship in their local communities. They have steadily made a position for themselves through their contributions to the development of the societies of their countries of residence (*zaijūkoku shakai*), and I cannot but feel great respect for the endeavors of these people. (*Kaigai Nikkeijin* no. 14, 10)

The election of second-generation Japanese Peruvian Alberto Fujimori as president of Peru in 1990 was a matter of great pride in Japan, at least before his autocratic style gave rise to mixed feelings. But in 1990, then Prime Minister Kaifu saw Fujimori's election as a kind of culmination, a final act of overcoming suffering that brought Nikkeijin into a glorious present:

> The emergence of a Japanese Peruvian as president of Peru provides us with a good opportunity to contemplate the sweat (*ase*), the tears (*namida*), and the glorious 120 plus years history of the Japanese emigrants (ijūsha) and Nikkeijin which continues to this day. (*Kaigai Nikkeijin* no. 29, 40)

Similar versions of the narrative of suffering and overcoming appear frequently in the greetings from prefectural governors that are printed on the first page of each issue of *Kaigai Nikkeijin* (Overseas Japanese), the journal published twice annually by the Association for Overseas Japanese. The statement of the governor of Kōchi Prefecture is noteworthy because he touches on so many of the stereotypes that are used to describe Japanese as well as Nikkeijin character and which are used in explanations of the recovery and triumph of the Japanese economy in the postwar period.

> Through their indomitable fighting spirit (*fukutsu no tōshi*), fortitude (*kigai*), perseverance (*nintai*), and their unceasing efforts (*fudan no doryoku*), the emigrants (*ijū sareta katagata*) to Central and South America conquered unimaginable hardships (*sōzō o zessuru konnan*) in a land where everything from climate, environment, language, and customs were different. That they have earned high regard for themselves, and have made numerous significant contributions to the development of the countries they moved to (*ijūsaki koku*), first in reinvigorating agriculture, as well as in politics, economics, and other

[33]

fields, is a source of great happiness, and deserves our deepest respect. (*Kaigai Nikkeijin* no. 14, 10)

The governor of Kōchi Prefecture acknowledged Nikkeijin as outstanding citizens of the countries to which they immigrated in a way that did not conflict with their continued identification with Japan. Nikkeijin were encouraged to be good citizens of their various countries and to act as Japan's informal diplomats, bridging cultural and physical differences to better Japan's international relations. As Basch, Glick Schiller, and Szanton Blanc have commented, "The significance of transmigrants to their country of origin in many ways rests on the extent of their incorporation into the national economy and political processes of their country of settlement" (Basch et al. 1994, 3).

In addition, the Kōchi governor and many others emphasized key character traits that linked Nikkeijin and Japanese. Perseverance (*nintai*) and effort (*doryoku*) in the face of unimaginable hardships (*sōzō o zessuru konnan*) were a favorite narrative of Japan, which rose up out of the ashes of World War II to become one of the world's economic superpowers. Although part of the motivation Japanese officials had for organizing the Nikkeijin conference in 1957 was their desire to apologize for the trouble that Nikkeijin had experienced during the war, by the 1980s this sense had been replaced by the narrative of suffering and overcoming that united Japanese and Nikkeijin.

In the context of the annual Nikkeijin conference, the constant repetition of the narrative emphasized the shared character and historical experience of Nikkeijin and Japanese. Like the story of identical twins who are separated at birth and grow up in very different environments but nevertheless develop uncanny similarities, the narrative of suffering and overcoming insisted that Japanese and Nikkeijin, at opposite ends of the world from each other, were deep down one and the same.

Practical and Impractical Nostalgia

The shared identity constructed at the conference drew on just a part of the symbolic resources Japanese and Nikkeijin had at their disposal. This sense of shared identity played a role in justifying preferential treatment of Nikkeijin in immigration policy that had facilitated the large-scale migration to Japan since 1989. However, both Japanese and Nikkeijin have been able to distinguish themselves from, as well as identify with, each other.

Almost none of the Nikkeijin working in Japanese factories attended the conference because it took place on weekdays. Nor was their participation solicited. Announcements for the conference did not appear in any of the Portuguese language newspapers published in Japan at the time, although several of their reporters did attend.[11] Edivaldo was working at the stamping presses as usual during the conference. He recoiled as I described the dinner reception at the prime minister's residence the second day, when one of the Japanese Brazilian representatives led the crowd of Nikkeijin participants and Japanese government officials in the rousing cheer *"Nihon koku banzai!"* ("Long live the Japanese nation!")—a cheer uncomfortably close to the wartime *"Nihon tei koku banzai!"* ("Long live the Japanese empire!"). He shook his head when I described his aunt's emotional response to the imperial presence.

Edivaldo's perspective was reflected in one critical and lengthy article in a Portuguese language weekly newspaper published in Japan. In this article, the journalist sarcastically suggested that the name of the conference be changed from the more inclusive Nikkeijin Taikai (Conference for Overseas Japanese) to Ijūsha Taikai (Conference for Japanese Migrants) (*Tudo Bem*, May 1995). He complained that the conference pandered to the nostalgic identification of first-generation immigrants and failed to address the most pressing issues (e.g. health care and accident compensation) facing younger Nikkeijin who were living and working in Japan.

Elderly Japanese immigrants living in Brazil have often constructed Japan as an object of nostalgic longing. When economic conditions spurred many young Japanese Brazilians to find work in Japan starting in the late 1980s, some went with their parents' and grandparents' idealized descriptions of Japan in mind. Once in Japan, however, they soon began to construct Brazil as the object of their patriotic identification. Local contexts where people live and work are often fraught with tension and inequality; in comparison, a distant homeland may appear in a favorable light. Identification with the distant, however, in itself did not preclude engagement in the immediate and local. Apparently apolitical, nostalgic constructions could be used in subtle ways to critique or to leverage local politics (see Battaglia 1995). The identification of older Nikkeijin with Japan during the conference may not have been solely an emotional expression of nostalgia, but also a practical one that critiqued conditions in Brazil and helped procure Japanese government aid for Japanese Brazilian institutions such as schools, hospitals, and nursing homes. For Edivaldo and other young Nikkeijin

---

[11] There were four Portuguese language weekly newspapers published in Japan while I was doing my fieldwork. *The International Press* and *Tudo Bem* were published in Tokyo. *Folha Mundial* and *Nova Visão* were published in Hamamatsu. All four were distributed nationwide wherever there was a concentration of Brazilian residents. *The International Press* eventually started television broadcasts and published a Spanish edition of the weekly newspaper. It also has the following web address: http://www.ipcdigital.com.

struggling in Japan, identification with Japan was misplaced because it did not engage in politics of the local issues facing Nikkeijin migrants in Japan. In the Japanese context, the saudade (yearning) that younger Nikkeijin expressed for a Brazilian homeland was a more pertinent critique of the discrimination they faced within the Japanese communities where they lived and worked.

[3]

On the Line at Yusumi Motors

In late November 1994, I moved into a company dormitory beside the Yusumi factory where I would work on the assembly line for three months. The dormitory was one of several drab three-story concrete buildings next to an expansive parking lot filled with rows of gleaming new sport utility vehicles, small pickup trucks, and minivans. The factory compound sprawled over more than seven hundred acres on the outskirts of town. Trucks ran up and down the service road, unloading parts along the length of the main factory building. Every now and then, a tractor trailer pulled out of the parking lot gates with a load of new cars destined for various dealerships in Japan and overseas. Across the road a pachinko parlor with its flickering multicolored neon sign beckoned workers to gamble their hard-earned wages. Next to the pachinko parlor stood a steak house and then nothing but open fields of stubble that remained from the rice harvest. A public bus ran up the road once an hour during the day. For insurance purposes, foreign workers were not allowed to own any transportation, and I imagined a routine of working, sleeping, eating, and playing pachinko.

On the day before I started work, I was given a tour of the dormitory by one of its administrators, Mr. Yoshida. All the rooms in my dorm were doubles, about 12 by 16 feet in area. They each came with a TV set, closet space to store the futons, a sink in the entranceway, and large sliding windows facing a courtyard. A florescent light hung from the low ceiling over the floor of six tatami mats. Without furniture, aside from a small television cabinet, the room appeared more spacious than it was. I was lucky not to be assigned a roommate.

Mr. Yoshida had retired from Yusumi at the normal age of fifty-five after many years of working on the line and now worked part-time in the dormitory at a much lower wage. He showed me the dining area, the laundry room, toilets, and the communal baths. The baths were at the far end of the first-floor hallway. We entered the dressing room that led into the bath room through a pair of glass doors. No one was using it at the time and I was able to peek inside. One end of the room was lined with spigots of hot and cold water where people could soap up and rinse off before soaking in the large rectangular bath. It overflowed with hot water, which filled the air with steam. Suddenly Mr. Yoshida ushered me back through the dressing room and out to the corridor. He had shown me the Japanese bath by mistake. I noticed a sign on the door that read *Nihonjin senyō* ("Japanese use only"). The entrance to the foreigners' bath was next door. The sign on this door read *Gaikokujin senyō* ("Foreigners' use only"). Inside was a smaller, older tub only half filled with tepid water. The firm's foreign trainees and Nikkeijin contract workers used this bath. My guide told me that I should use it as well.

At the Conference for Overseas Japanese, Japanese and Nikkeijin constructed and celebrated a shared identity. In Japanese workplaces, however, Nikkeijin were often categorized as foreigners. Nikkeijin were generally hired through intermediary employment brokers—terms of employment that put Nikkeijin in a distinctly marginal position in relation to Japanese workers. At Yusumi, some Nikkeijin were hired on short-term contracts and were mostly housed in a separate dormitory apart from Japanese employees. Those who resided in primarily Japanese dormitories were segregated in the bathing arrangements. Although Nikkeijin generally preferred to take showers rather than to soak in the hot tub and thus did not seem to mind the segregation, the arrangement symbolically reinforced their marginal position within the firm and the larger labor market. The marginalization of Nikkeijin within the labor market simultaneously reflected and created feelings of distinction Japanese workers and management held in relation to Nikkeijin.

Nikkeijin were not the only foreigners present within the factory. The Yusumi corporation produced a significant number of cars for export, and has developed numerous overseas joint ventures in Asia, North and South America, and Europe. Many Japanese supervisors and administrators have spent time abroad setting up plants, and Yusumi factories frequently hosted foreign trainees (*kenshūsei*) from their overseas joint ventures. Despite the auto industry's increasingly global integration of capital, production, and distribution, however, a curiously local discourse emerged among Japanese managers, academics, and bureaucrats; the discourse centered on work ethic and responsibility toward the firm. These were qualities that the broader Japanese media in the recessionary 1990s indicated were vanishing in Japan. Even as the vaunted "Japanese employment system" with its three pillars of lifetime employment (shūshin koyō), seniority wages (nenkō joretsu), and company-based unions (as opposed to trade unions) appeared to be collapsing, some Japanese portrayed foreigners as self-interested and sloppy workers, lacking the qualities necessary for full integration within Japanese workplace communities.

Japanese often criticized Nikkeijin and other foreign workers as sloppy, irresponsible, and lacking in loyalty toward the firm. In so doing, Japanese workers distracted themselves from their own ambivalent feelings about their firm. Japanese workers' narratives suggested that their sense of identification with their firms varied according to the recognition they had received over the years in the form of promotions. Only a small number of workers achieved their career goals within Yusumi's competitive workplace environment. This dissatisfaction with their careers did not translate into solidarity with recently arrived foreign workers, however. On the contrary, the foreign presence prompted some of the Japanese to attach themselves to an older discourse of loyalty and responsibility despite their feeling that their firm did not always reward these values.

Inside the Factory

In 1993 Yusumi Motors employed more than 14,000 workers in its six factories and various offices and employed many tens of thousands more in its numerous parts suppliers. It was one of the largest firms in Hamamatsu and was central to the city's economy. Unlike some of the other large manufacturers, which avoided hiring Nikkeijin as well as other foreigners, Yusumi had hired a large number for its factories. My introduction to Yusumi Motors came through a friend of a friend of a friend—a middle-aged Japanese man who had grown up in Hamamatsu and had childhood friends in administrative positions at several major manufacturers in town. He ran a small English language school and relied on his connections to establish language training accounts with these firms. He was generous enough to arrange an interview for me with Yusumi managers. During this interview, I requested permission to conduct participant observation in the factory. I explained my position as a student of anthropology and Japanese workplace organization. The company hired me for an initial three-month contract on the condition that I pulled my weight and worked like everyone else. One of my interviewers said that the work would be hard, and that I would not receive special privileges as a researcher. He reassured me, however, that I would probably be able to handle the work since I was still young (I was twenty-nine). He told me that the average age of Brazilians working on the line at the plant was twenty-six; the average for all line workers was about thirty, and the average for the plant as a whole, including line and office workers and administrators, was thirty-six.

On my first day of work I showed up in my bright new blue and white uniform at the factory's main offices at 7:50 A.M. Chimes went off at five minutes before the hour. People sat at their desks in dim morning light that filtered through the windows until the office lights came on at 8:10. I was introduced to an elderly man named Nakano, who gave me a brief overview of Yusumi, its factories, and what each of them produced. He also ran through a list of principles to which all Yusumi workers were expected to adhere: safety *(anzen)*, orderliness *(seiri)*, tidiness *(seiton)*, maintenance *(seibi)*, and organization *(seizen)*. Banners and stickers promoting "Safety first" *(anzen dai'ichi)* decorated the factory.

After a brief visit to the factory health clinic, where a doctor and nurse checked my blood pressure and listened to my heart, I had an early lunch in the cafeteria, and then got to go on a tour of the plant. Little unmanned trolleys that pulled cartloads of car parts to the workstations played a simple tune and flashed warning lights as they rolled slowly up and down the walkways. When these trolleys arrived at their workstations, they would automatically detach the carts and continue down the walkways and back to the parts supply areas. The cavernous space of the factory was filled with scaffolding upon which bare light bulbs and bony machinery were suspended. The tunes of the trolleys mixed with various factory sounds—the cacophony of specialized machines at each workstation, the whirring of hundreds of air guns that workers used to attach parts to vehicle frames, and the constant creaking of the assembly line as it snaked through the factory. Later that day, my section chief gave me a pair of earplugs.

There were two main assembly lines at the plant. Workers assembled pickup trucks and minivans on Line One. They assembled two types of recreational vehicles on Line Two. When I was there, Line One comprised about 120 workstations *(kōtei)*, and workers churned out between 320 and 400 vehicles per shift, depending on the production targets for a particular month. Line Two had about 100 workstations and produced a somewhat smaller number of vehicles per shift. Most workstations were staffed by one worker, and for every ten or twelve workstations there was a section chief *(hanchō)*. The section chief had to know the tasks of each workstation under his supervision, responding whenever one of his workers pulled on a yellow cord that set off a siren and flashed the number of the workstation on a large board. I made heavy use of the yellow cord my first two weeks on the job. Next to the yellow cord hung a red one, which I was told to pull only in life-threatening circumstances, as it would bring the entire line with about 120 workstations to a halt.

Composition of the Workforce

In 1994 and 1995, the factory where I worked was staffed by about 2,500 employees. There were three major sections to the plant—welding, paint, and assembly—of which assembly had by far the greatest number of workers. Most of the work in the welding section was done by robots. The few people who worked there were primarily responsible for supplying parts to these robots and maintaining them. To a lesser degree, automation had also decreased the numbers of people in the paint section. The intricacy of the tasks in the assembly section, however, made automation less profitable there. The significant change in the assembly section was in the composition of the workforce. Until the mid-1980s, there had been almost no foreigners in the plant. When I was there, about five hundred of the plant's 2,500 workers were foreigners. Table 3.1 provides the breakdown of employment status for Japanese, Nikkeijin, and other foreigners. The numbers in the table are my estimates; the actual numbers fluctuated over the three months I was there.

There were about 100 women working at the plant. Some of the younger ones were clerical workers in the administrative offices. Older women worked inside the factory, supplying parts to each of the workstations along the line during the day shifts. A handful of young women worked day shifts on the line itself, side by side with men in assembly. Most women were hired either as part-time staff or as contract workers. A number of younger women who worked in the offices were hired on a full-time basis. Most such hires left or switched to part-time status upon marriage or the birth of a child (see Roberts 1994; Ogasawara 1998, 63–8).

Spotting the foreign workers was easy: they wore yellow hard hats while Japanese wore white ones. I got to wear a white one because no yellow ones were available when I started work. This caused an occasional visiting engineer or worker from another part of the line to mistake me for Japanese. During my employment, Yusumi hired about fifty Nikkeijin directly on six-

Table 3.1. Employment Status in the Yusumi Plant (January 1995)

	Japanese	Nikkeijin	Other foreigners
Permanent employees	2,000 (20 women)	0	0
Contract workers	80 (20 women)	50	0
Part-time workers	40 (all women)	0	0
Subcontract workers	0	250 (20 women)	0
Trainees	0	0	220°

Note: All figures refer to male employees unless otherwise noted.

°Trainees included Koreans, Chinese, Indians, and Pakistanis.

[41]

month renewable contracts. In the late 1980s and early 1990s, Yusumi representatives had gone to Brazil to recruit Nikkeijin, but by the time I started working there in 1994, it was able to recruit most from the large pool of Nikkeijin already in Japan.

In addition to the fifty Nikkeijin hired on renewable short-term contracts, there were about 250 Nikkeijin working for in-house subcontractors on the perimeters of the main factory building. These workers wore uniforms that clearly distinguished them from Yusumi employees. In contrast to Nikkeijin hired by Yusumi on contract, almost all of the Nikkeijin who worked for subcontractors had been hired indirectly by employment brokers. Although these brokers paid their Nikkeijin workers slightly better hourly wages than did Yusumi, the brokers did not bother enrolling their workers in accident and health insurance plans or in pension plans.[1]

The 220 trainees included members of Yusumi's Korean, Chinese, Indian, and Pakistani joint ventures. There were about 100 Korean, 50 Chinese, 50 Indian, and 20 Pakistani trainees the months I worked there. Trainees worked on the line for three to six months, receiving stipends that were well below Japanese minimum wages, but were given health insurance, transportation, and lodging. Of the twelve workers in my section when I started, two were Chinese. They returned to China two months later and were replaced by two Koreans. The factory shut down for winter holidays from December 29 through January 5. When I returned to work on January 6, ninety-seven Korean trainees were starting a six-month stint. All of them had just been hired by a large Korean maker with which Yusumi had a joint technology development program. Japanese commented that of all the foreign workers in the plant, the Koreans were the best. Most of them were in their mid-twenties, and many were hardened from having just completed three years of military service. They had strength, stamina, and discipline, and so took to line work quickly. In addition, some Japanese noted that Koreans were motivated by the desire to prove to the Japanese that they were their equals or better.

Working on the Line

Mr. Nakano ended my tour of the factory by introducing me to my new section chief, Kimata Masamichi, who assigned me to spend the rest of the day at workstation #46. There I found a twenty-one-year-old Japanese worker from Hokkaido. His hair was dyed reddish brown. In one earlobe were planted several studs, and a thin cross dangled below them. I was to

---

[1] I discuss the system of employment brokers in greater detail in chapter 4.

The Chinese trainee at workstation #45

take his place in a couple of days when he moved to the engine line. I spent most of my first day watching and trying to figure out how he got everything done as the relentless line of pickups and minivans pushed forward. He was a blur of motion. The primary job at this workstation was installing air filters and tubing, but there were many other odds and ends as well. For pickups, he had to insert plastic tabs that would secure wiring or tubing farther down the line. He also had to fasten together electric wires that ran near the radiator fan so they would not get sucked into the fan.

The two types of vehicles that moved down the line came in a variety of models, each of which required somewhat different procedures in assembly. There were different filters to install depending on whether the car had air-conditioning and whether it was destined for cold or hot climates. A special filter for turbo engines required extra bolting. The different filters had been arranged on the carts that the trolleys brought to my workstation in an order corresponding with the specifications for the vehicles coming along the line.

I tried several parts of the job individually, but could not imagine being able to do them all together at the speed the line was moving. A few seconds was an eternity on the assembly line. A fast worker had time to check for mistakes or to refill the various bins of bolts, washers, screws, tabs, and other parts that lined one side of his workstation. If a worker appeared to have too much time on his hands, however, the section chief would add an extra task to his station, so most people tried to look busy. Someone who was just one second slow was always working frantically into the next workstation, often interfering with his neighbor's work, and then rushing back to the head of his own workstation to start on the next vehicle.

After two days, a short and skinny Japanese worker who looked about fifty years old was assigned to train me at my station. He was not so familiar with my workstation and could not do the job with the same quiet intensity as the younger worker with the earrings had. He noted that the line was much faster now than it had been twenty years previously. The next day another quiet, thoughtful-looking young man named Kato replaced the older man. Kato stayed with me for a week, after which I had to work on my own. The assembly line doubled back several times, and the quality-control inspectors stationed at the end of the line were just across from my workstation. When they periodically yelled "Kato!" I knew that I had screwed something on a little crookedly or had failed to secure some wires properly. Kato would hurry over there and return with instructions on how to improve my workmanship. Some people could conquer their jobs faster than others depending on their dexterity, experience, and the speed of the line at the time.

Although I was left to myself after one week, it took several more for me to master my workstation. Initially, I hated the vans because they took more time. Vans usually came down the line once for every two trucks, but with each one I lost a little ground, until finally I had to pull the yellow cord, calling the section chief over to help me catch up. It was important that I left nothing undone at my station because the engine was installed at the next station, making it very difficult or impossible to install my parts afterward.

The production target for November was very high. Each shift on Line One was to assemble about four hundred vehicles, which amounted to just one minute and twenty-four seconds per vehicle. In December, the daily production goal dropped to about 350 vehicles per shift, giving us an additional sixteen seconds per vehicle. This completely changed the character of the work. December was almost tranquil in contrast to November, when people had run about frantically and sirens wailed continuously as workers pulled on yellow cords to get assistance from their section chiefs. Management did not consult with the union when they made decisions to increase line speed. Several of my Japanese coworkers complained about the top-down quality of these decisions. When production goals were increased, some section chiefs tried to rouse their workers' fighting spirit (*gambaru seishin*) to meet the challenge, but most workers—Japanese and foreign alike—just resigned themselves to getting through the day. On the last day of the year, the factory chief (*kōjōchō*) thanked us at the morning assembly for having assembled 170,000 vehicles on the pickup truck and minivan line that year and 110,000 on the sport utility vehicle line.

Aside from the period when there was someone to help train or assist me at my workstation, for nine and one-half hours every workday (including Saturdays every other week) I was normally too busy to talk to anyone. Moreover, the noise in the factory made it difficult to speak to even workers in adjacent workstations. Sometimes when I was falling behind and working desperately on a truck that had already passed into the next workstation, Alex Saito, the Japanese Peruvian into whose space I had encroached, would shout questions at me in Spanish: "What's America like?" "Have you been to California?" "How much does a car cost in America?" All I could do most times was smile nervously and rush back to my area to start work on the next truck moving overhead. Alex had been working at the plant for almost three years and was in complete command of his workstation, where engines were attached to the bodies of the vehicles. To relieve his boredom, Alex would sometimes play with controls for the adjustable platform on which the engines were mounted, jerking it up and down, left and right, but always centering it just in time to slip the engine right into place.

There were two shifts at the factory. One started at 7:00 A.M. and ended at 5:20 P.M. The other started at 5:20 P.M. and ended at 3:40 A.M. Each shift had a forty-five-minute break for lunch or dinner, plus three five-minute rest breaks. All told, line workers spent about ten and a half hours a day in

[45]

the factory. During rest breaks I would sometimes join the members of my work section in our rest area suspended over the assembly line. There, people watched TV, smoked, and sipped tea or drank canned coffee or vitamin drinks they had bought from one of the vending machines on the factory floor. If the rest area was too smoky, I would join Alex, who would spread cardboard on the soiled carpet underneath the assembly line. Lying on his back, staring up at the dark roof of the factory, he daydreamed about the cattle ranch he would buy when he went back to Peru.

Alex would often have his lunch with a young, quiet, long-haired Japanese worker from a section in which he had previously worked, but most Japanese and foreigners sat in segregated groups. Nationality, age, and gender all tended to determine seating patterns. A group of seven or eight young Brazilian men often sat together, joking with each other about their haircuts and girlfriends. On day shifts they would point out women about whom others at their table supposedly fantasized. One group of somewhat older workers (mid-thirties to early forties) included one Peruvian Nikkeijin along with a couple of Brazilians. The Peruvian was suspicious of whether Alex and some of the younger Peruvians really had any Japanese "blood." Alex's brother had apparently married a Nikkeijin and had arranged to "adopt" Alex on paper. Although this older Peruvian was "pure Nikkeijin" (*Nikkeijin puro*), he did not speak Japanese as well as some of the "mestizos" or "falsos" who, perhaps because of the suspicions about their backgrounds, had made greater efforts to learn Japanese.

Sometimes I ate with Japanese from my work section, but they generally finished quickly and returned early to the rest area by the assembly line. I would then shift to one or another group of Nikkeijin, and sometimes to a group of Indian trainees, a few of whom spoke some English. I had little means of communicating with the Chinese or Korean trainees who sat at their own tables, and just gave them a friendly nod or smile when they passed. Dietary restrictions of the Indians forced management to train cooks to prepare special vegetarian dishes for them. The cooks also made some effort to cater to Chinese and Korean palates. The Chinese could not stomach the cold rice lunches favored by Japanese and often patronized the hot noodle counter. The cafeteria also offered Korean side dishes of kimchi and other pickled vegetables.

By December, we could see our breath as we worked in the mornings. The space heaters suspended from the scaffolding over the workstations dried the air more than warmed it. During this time—but unrelated to the cold—I developed repetitive stress injury, which I learned was common among workers on the assembly line. I would wake up in the morning and my fingers would be frozen in a curled position. They would not open even after I ran warm water over them, and they felt as if they would snap if I

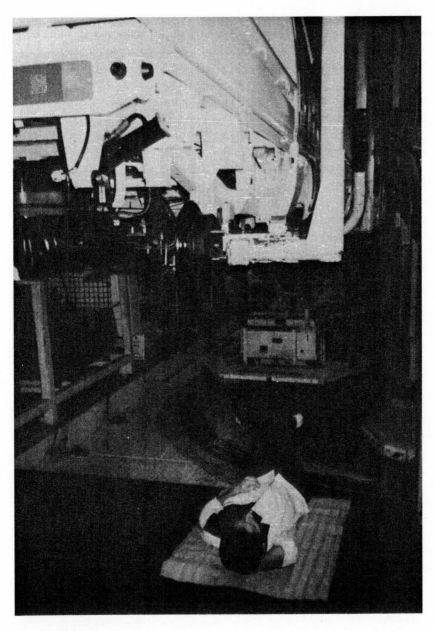

Alex during break time

tried to force them straight. I tried rubbing menthol balm over the joints of my fingers and sleeping with gloves on, but this did little to help.

When I went to the factory's clinic during lunchtime, the doctor gave me a painkilling cream that loosened the joints of my fingers. One middle-aged Japanese seasonal worker from Hokkaido told me that his hands hurt so badly he would wake up at night. He said he did not use the cream much because it only helped temporarily and apparently had bad side effects if used too often. A young Japanese worker told me it took almost a year from the time he started working before the pain in his hands subsided.

The state of my fingers made me worry whether I would be able to do my job, especially when it was so cold in the factory. They were still stiff at the start of the day, but once the line started moving, my fingers warmed up quickly enough for me to keep up. It was strange that precisely the work that had produced my condition was what brought my fingers back to life each morning, as if they had signed a contract to function only for the benefit of Yusumi. My condition persisted during the three months I worked at Yusumi and disappeared shortly after I quit.

Feelings about Foreign Workers

The relative wages of Japanese and Nikkeijin were a major source of complaint among Japanese workers. One young Japanese worker, Yoneda Masaru, said it bothered him to know that people with no experience got paid as much as he did. He also said foreign trainees got breaks that Japanese workers could not expect. He complained that even though his fingers hurt him his first year of work at Yusumi, "people who enter as full-time employees have no choice but to work whether or not they are in pain. Managers can't force Chinese or Indians to work like that. Managers realize that foreign workers can't do quite as much. Japanese force each other to work until they can achieve production goals."

In January, I moved from the workstation where I had installed air filters to a new one where I installed front right drive shafts and wheels. This workstation required me to learn how to use a completely different set of tools, and it took me about two weeks again to get up to speed. Shimada, the Japanese worker assigned to help me as I developed my skills, did so grudgingly. He felt toward me the kind of resentment Masaru had described Japanese workers feeling toward foreigners who were paid highly despite their inability to pull their weight. Shimada thought I did not try hard enough to learn the tasks at the new workstation, and I overheard him tell my section chief, Kimata, that I could do the job on my own if I was motivated (*yaru ki ga areba*). After one week, I could complete three or four consecutive vehicles on my own, losing some ground with each one and finally having to call for help. Every time Shimada came over, he would accuse me of not really trying, sometimes coming up directly behind me as I worked on the next car and literally breathing down my neck as he asked me if I was hurrying (*Isoideiru ka?*). On other occasions, he told me that I was spoiled (*amaeteiru*) to expect that someone would always be there to help me out.

Shimada tried to pressure me into speeding up in various ways. One time, he asked me how I would feel if I were working alone opposite someone who had a helper assigned to him.[2] I said I would not mind. He said he would be angry. He added that since I was earning a good salary, I should pull my weight. I responded that at the start, no one could keep up with the speed of the line. He said that full-time workers initially earned apprenticeship (*minarai*) wages, which were less than regular wages, but that I was getting more than a full wage. He speculated that I must be getting 300,000 yen per month.[3] This made me laugh, since my last paycheck had allowed me to take home only 170,000 yen. He said he had gotten only 140,000.[4] Shimada maintained that in Japan, I should live by Japanese rules and not expect special treatment. I agreed, pointing out that I had made steady improvement, sometimes able to do five cars consecutively when the previous day I had always needed help after only three or four. *"Mittomonai!"* ("Disgraceful!") he muttered as he stalked away.

Shimada and Masaru both felt that foreigners should be held to the same standards as Japanese workers and that no one should be exempted from the demands of "Japanese rules." These rules included a prescription to act responsibly—to earn one's wages. They felt that foreign workers received more compensation than they deserved. Many younger Japanese workers were in fact frustrated by their own wages and prospects for promotion (see

[2] A Japanese worker installed front left drive shafts and wheels directly opposite from where I mounted the front right parts.

[3] At the exchange rate of roughly 100 yen to the dollar, this worked out to $3,000.

[4] These figures were for December, when we worked fewer days than in an average month. Contract workers and recent hires earned between 230,000 and 240,000 yen on an average month, calculating in the annual bonuses. Having been at Yusumi for about four years, Shimada was probably earning somewhat more than contract workers. Over the three-month period of my contract, I worked a total of 560 hours. My gross income for this period was 898,000 yen, or 1,604 yen per hour, 55 percent more than my basic wage rate of 1,038 yen per hour. About half of the difference came from the legally obligatory 25 percent wage premiums for overtime and nighttime hours and Saturdays, as well as premiums for working an alternate-shift schedule. The rest of the difference came in the form of the 20,000 yen bonuses for perfect attendance in any month, a year-end bonus of 50,000 yen, and an end-of-contract bonus calculated at 1,000 yen for each working day for those who had missed less than 5 percent of days during the contract period. After income taxes, health insurance (*shakai hoken*), and pension (*kōsei nenkin*) premiums were deducted from my paychecks, however, I ended up earning the equivalent of 1,262 yen per hour, or 236,000 per month. At 10,000 yen per month, the dormitory where I stayed was a bargain.

Roberson 1998, 125–6), a frustration that expressed itself in their critique of foreign workers.

Younger Permanently Employed Workers

The Yusumi union's booklet "Reassuring Life Plan" *(Anshin Raifu Puran)* identifies the following major life events: entering the firm, marriage, having one's own house, having children, children's education through college, children's weddings, and finally retirement. As Yusumi company union representatives explained to me, the seniority wage policy took into account increasing financial responsibilities that accompany major stages of the life course. The seniority wage system meant that starting wages were low, and that the discrepancy between the wages of two permanent Japanese doing identical work may be large if one was recently hired and the other was at the end of his career. Compounding this, some of the young Japanese workers I knew complained that since 1992, the recession had kept their annual seniority wage increases to insignificant levels. Their wages had started low and seemed to stay there.

There was a high turnover rate among newly hired "permanent" employees. A guidance counselor at Hamamatsu Kōgyō Kōkō, a vocational high school, told me that in 1991, Yusumi hired 480 workers, of whom 168 quit within a year. In 1992, the company hired 473 workers, of whom 127 quit within a year. In 1993, Yusumi hired 495 workers, of whom 113 quit within a year. The rate at which new hires quit within a year declined from 35 percent in 1991, to 27 percent in 1992, to 23 percent in 1993, possibly reflecting the onset of recession and a growing concern about the possibility of finding other work for comparable pay.

These separation rates were consistent with those Kazuo Koike found in his 1983 study of separation rates in Japanese firms. Even at large manufacturing firms (defined as having more than one thousand employees), he found that the separation rate was more than 20 percent annually for the first five years of employment, after which it dropped below 10 percent (Koike 1983, 40–2). This meant that the majority (roughly 70 percent) of new workers left their firms within five years of starting. High turnover among young workers at large firms was normal, and turnover at smaller manufacturing firms was generally even higher (Nomura 1994, 40; Roberson 1998, chap. 7).

Yusumi hired people for semiskilled manufacturing jobs with the understanding that most of them would last no more than a few years. This served at least two purposes: to give the firm a way to have a high proportion of workers at the low end of the wage scale, and to screen out less dedicated workers before they earned seniority. The logic was similar to that which other writers have described with regard to female secretarial and blue-collar staff (Brinton 1992; Roberts 1996; Roberson 1998, chap. 6). In many firms, women were expected to leave work upon marriage, which was often only a few years after they had started work. If they returned to work after their children were old enough for school, they would start back again as part-time employees whose wages did not rise with seniority. High turnover reduced payroll outlays, and there was considerable pressure on women to quit after several years. Some pressure was applied in disguised forms such as marriage bonuses management offered for women who left for that reason. Pressure to quit was packaged as expression of concern for the personal futures of female employees. Similarly, at Yusumi, management could argue that it was natural for a certain percentage of young workers to discover that they were not meant for factory work and to explore other options.

Informal pressure on workers to quit was not the only explanation for the high rates of attrition. In the previous decade, the status of factory work had fallen steadily among young people, possibly leading more of them to take such jobs only on a temporary basis. The recent depiction in the popular press of factory work as dangerous, dirty, and difficult (in Japanese referred to as the three Ks: *kiken, kitanai, kitsui*) indicated that positive artisanal qualities attributed to factory work at certain times in the past (see Kondo 1990, chap. 7) had eroded considerably.[5] As more foreign workers continued to enter factory jobs in Japan, some Japanese increasingly associated certain kinds of factory work with foreigners, as work inappropriate for respectable Japanese.

Large Japanese companies offered the ideology of lifetime employment and security but benefited from the vast majority of new entries who quit voluntarily before gaining the seniority that brings higher wages. Masaru had been at Yusumi four and a half years when I met him. He was twenty-two, having entered the firm straight out of high school. He told me that about 100 others had started at the plant the same year. About half dropped out during the first year, several more quitting each year until only twenty still remained when I interviewed him.

One of the major reasons people he knew quit was that factory work proved less lucrative than they had been led to believe. A high school guidance counselor in charge of helping students find employment provided the information in Table 3.2, which details the package Yusumi offered the

[5]Thomas Smith notes that modern industrial factory work had low status in Japan around the turn of the century (1988: 239–41). The spread of factory work and the success of the union movement in improving conditions in the 1920s and in the early postwar period made factory work much more acceptable (Gordon 1985). More recently, however, the status of factory work seems to be in decline.

1995 crop of high school graduates. In addition, permanent workers received significant bonuses every six months. These summer and winter bonuses together could amount to about five and one-half months of base salary. Recent employees also received the option of living in the subsidized dormitories. Although the compensation was not bad, it was not particularly rewarding considering the demanding nature of the work and the number of hours that had to be put in.

Another young Japanese worker, Nakata Kenichi, had been with the firm for seven years since graduating from high school in faraway Yamaguchi Prefecture, but said he had thought of quitting countless times. When production was high in 1992, and contract employees, most of whom were Brazilians and Peruvians, were earning high hourly wages plus much more for long overtime hours, he had considered quitting and being rehired as a contract employee *(keiyaku shain)*. Almost all such contracts were for six months and thus had no implicit guarantee of permanent employment. Moreover, contract workers did not receive seniority wage increases, biannual bonuses, or promotions. There were a handful of Japanese contract workers, although most of them were holdovers from an earlier time when agricultural workers from colder regions came to work in factories during the slack season. Despite these drawbacks, Kenichi said that during the boom years in the early 1990s, many contract employees could save up to three hundred thousand yen per month, far more than he had been able to save.

Kenichi and Masaru suggested several other reasons that many young Japanese employees had quit work at Yusumi. One was a general dislike of the day-and-night alternating-shift system. Also, adjusting to a rigid work schedule was difficult after relatively less demanding years in school. In some cases, personal conflicts with section chiefs had stymied workers' chances for promotion. Some left to find work closer to their hometowns. Some found simply that they did not like working on the line. Some re-

Table 3.2. Entry-level Wages and Deductions for Entry-level Yusumi Employees (1995)

154,000	yen monthy base salary (roughly $1,540)
+ 30,727	*kōsan* (compensation for day/night alternate-shift schedule)
+ 20,595	*zangyō* (estimated overtime pay)
= 205,322	gross wage
− 20,268	*shakai hoken* (health and pension plan)
− 6,810	income tax
− 2,000	lodging (not discounted for those who commute from home)
= 176,244	take-home pay (roughly $1,762)

quested transfers to different workstations and quit when these requests were denied.

For others, the work alternately offered disappointment and hope. "I'd liked cars since I was small and wanted a job where I could work with them. But I didn't realize I'd be working on the line all the time," Kenichi explained. Recently, however, patience seemed to have born him fruit. He was taken off the line to work in the maintenance section and was responsible for repairing any machine in the entire assembly division that had trouble. The new assignment was much more varied and challenging than his previous work. It normally took two years to master all the skills demanded of workers in the maintenance section, but he had set a goal of learning them all in just one year. The old nagging doubts about his future at Yusumi had disappeared.

Masaru was still planning to quit within one year. He said that he might have quit earlier if he had not taken out a loan to buy a car. Without assurance of finding a comparably paying job, he had decided to continue working until he paid off the loan; in the meantime, however, he was given a small promotion. He became what is called a "helper" *(herupā)*. Every work section had both a section chief and a helper. He was rotated through all of the workstations within his section so that he could take anyone's place in case someone was absent. Of his entering cohort, only two others had become helpers. He admitted he was lucky in that the position had in effect been left to him to fill; the others who had joined his section earlier and were ahead of him in line for the position had all quit. Nevertheless, helpers received no more than other line workers in salary, and there was no guarantee that they would be able to make the next significant step up to section chief. Although the occasional move from one workstation to another was a reprieve from the mentally numbing routine at a single station, helpers, unlike section chiefs, were almost always on the line somewhere. Like Kenichi, Masaru had been a car enthusiast during high school, but now was considering "taking a 180-degree turn and doing something completely unrelated to cars." He said most of the friends he had at Yusumi who quit had left the auto industry altogether.

Other Permanently Employed Workers

Attrition rates among older workers at Yusumi were not nearly as high as they were among recent hires. The longer that one worked at a firm with a seniority wage policy, the greater the incentives to continue doing so. Older Japanese employees in general did not express the same kind of frustration about wages in comparison to foreign workers' that younger ones did. Long years of employment with the firm did not indicate a worker's identification with the firm, however. My section chief, Kimata, revealed some of the frustrations he felt about his career at Yusumi. His feelings suggest that success in promotion may affect the way workers identify with their work and their firms.

Kimata Masamichi

At age fifty-three, Kimata was just two years from the mandatory retirement age and earned a much higher salary than the recent hires and contract workers. Kimata had a good reputation among foreign workers. Several Indian trainees as well as Alex Saito, the Peruvian Nikkeijin, told me that Kimata was fair and helpful. He bore no grudges against foreign workers, although he could at times be critical of them for sloppiness in their work. He took pride in the Japanese work culture. He was not content with his position in Yusumi, however, and during the three months that I worked with him, he expressed his frustration with Yusumi management and life in Japan more generally in various subtle ways.

For example, Kimata often spoke fondly of the year he spent in Canada in the late 1980s when Yusumi was setting up a joint venture factory there. He would often linger at my section, reminiscing about how much larger and less expensive houses were in Canada and how playing golf was so inexpensive that he had played practically every week in which snow did not cover the ground. He remembered losing golf balls in the dandelions in the spring and in the maple leaves in the autumn. I asked Kimata if the Yusumi plant in Canada was very different from those in Japan. He said that in the Canadian plant, there was often enough space between vehicles on the line for workers to read the newspaper and to sip their coffee. Kimata said the Canadian men were rippling with muscles but they could not compete with Japanese when it came to working on the line. In addition, the assembly lines in Canada were not as flexible. Both of the lines in our plant in Hamamatsu handled two types of vehicles. The lines in Canada could take only one type of vehicle at a time. A siren would often intrude on Kimata's commentaries, sending him hurrying down the line and leaving me alone again to my tasks.

While Kimata took pride in certain aspects of Japanese workplace culture, he lamented the fact that workers no longer socialized with each other. The one time Yusumi workers did socialize was at the year-end party *(bōnenkai)*—an institution at many firms and in many informal groups and clubs throughout Japan. Kimata had informed me that our work section would have its yearend party in early December. I had already made plans to go to Tokyo immediately after work that day and could not attend. When I saw him the following week, Kimata told me that they had had a good time even though only four of the ten members of our work section had gone. I apologized again for not going. Kimata suggested that the lack of team spirit was not confined to our work section. Despite the stereotype of community in Japanese firms, Kimata said that people got together after work in Canada much more than at Yusumi. He explained that since the police had cracked down on drunk driving, they did not go out much anymore in Hamamatsu. Employees caught by police for drunken driving could even lose their jobs. As a carmaker, Yusumi was very concerned about how an employee's driving record might affect the company image. Section chiefs often made safe driving the topic of speeches at morning meetings, especially the week before a holiday weekend. As important as the strict policy was, Kimata regretted its effects on fraternization among coworkers. He said that when he was younger, he used to go out quite a bit with his colleagues. Things had been different then.

Kimata's fond recollections of Canadian lifestyles and earlier times in Japan often disguised a critique of Yusumi management. He would occasionally express his dissatisfaction more directly. One such occasion came several days after the president and several other top Yusumi administrators toured the factory. We had spent extra effort the day before their visit tidying our workstations. It all seemed to pass without incident until several days later, when we came to work and found that all the coiled air hoses attached to our power tools had been shortened. These hoses had been able to stretch a certain distance to give the workers greater flexibility as the vehicles moved down the line. The administrators had apparently thought that the hoses looked too long, but in shortening them, they reduced the window of opportunity workers had for attaching a given part, and many workers ran into trouble. If we fell behind for any reason, we were forced to detach our tools from their hoses and reattach the tools to other hoses farther down the line to catch up with the car as it kept moving. These extra procedures made it ever more difficult to keep up. Many workers were forced to pull on their yellow cords, filling the factory with sirens and flashing lights. Kimata muttered how stupid the managers were for ordering the hoses shortened. The next day, he took the initiative of changing most of them back to the old ones.

Kimata looked after the workers in his section. If he had helped me catch up, he would often see if he could help the workers nearby as well. When the bins of nuts and bolts were running low at the next workstation, where a Chinese trainee was stationed, Kimata would replace them with full bins from the stack by the service aisle alongside the assembly line. Workers could do this themselves, but it made the work easier when Kimata did it. The Japanese worker stationed just opposite the trainee almost never said a word to anyone, and he never asked Kimata for help. Because of his silence, I could not tell if he felt resentment toward me or the Chinese trainee for frequently calling for help, or toward Kimata for complying with our requests. Kimata was sensitive and smart to show this man a certain amount of attention, thereby defusing whatever resentment he may have felt.

Kimata complained about still being stuck on the factory floor after almost thirty years with the company. He had not gotten very far at Yusumi, he explained, because he had not started there directly out of school. He had started in his mid-twenties, after spending several years with a different firm in Tokyo. I sensed Kimata's frustration in his attitude toward his immediate superior, the group leader (*kumichō*). When I asked Kimata about the kumichō, he told me that he was more of a walker than a worker. All he did was walk up and down the aisles, never getting his hands dirty helping out on the line. Whereas section chiefs were responsible for between ten and thirteen workers, often helping out directly with the line work itself, the kumichō had jurisdiction over several sections, and I doubt that any kumichō did much actual assembly work. Still, the kumichō should have had a good grasp of the details of assembly work, and Kimata suggested that our kumichō did not.

Kimata felt lucky to be nearing retirement. This was in part because he felt his ability had not been properly recognized and rewarded. He also sensed that he had been at the company during the golden days of the industry, and that those days were over. Even though Kimata had not gotten as far in his career as he had hoped, he wondered whether the younger workers today would attain even that much. He mentioned several other plants in town that had relocated to China. Indeed, the presence of Chinese trainees at Yusumi was an indication that this could happen to our factory in the near future. Although production at Yusumi's joint ventures in China and India were aimed at those two growing markets, many of their vehicles had the potential to be reverse-imported to Japan as well. The urge to do just that would increase if the numerous joint ventures in Asia established more production capacity than the growing middle classes there could utilize.

Talking with me, Kimata switched back and forth between expressing pride in the Japanese worker and wistfully reminiscing about the good life in Canada. He seemed somewhat discontented with the drudgery of his Japanese lifestyle and was frustrated in his desire for promotion. Once he even told me that he wished he had been born Canadian, but he brushed aside my question when I asked him if he thought about buying a house in Canada and retiring there. In the end, his dream of a better life in Canada seemed to be more a critique of Yusumi rather than a desire or intention to actually leave Yusumi. During one of the five-minute breaks when the members of our section had crowded in our little enclosed rest area, the TV news reported that Otowa Nobuko, a Japanese actress, had just died at the age of seventy. Kimata joked that he would like to die at that age. He was considering working five years past the official retirement age, until sixty, and playing pachinko for another ten years after that. Then, making a sudden gesture with his shoulders and wrists, he demonstrated the sudden way that he hoped to die.

Hinoki Kazunori

Hinoki's career at Yusumi resembled Kimata's to a great extent. They both had started work there a little less than thirty years ago. Before joining Yusumi, both had worked elsewhere for a number of years. Looking back on his career, however, Hinoki exuded much greater satisfaction than Kimata. After two interviews of roughly two hours each with Hinoki, I realized that there were still many things he had glossed over or left unspoken. His responses to my questions were in many ways packaged as precepts to live by, intended for my benefit as someone who, in his eyes, was just starting out in life. Nevertheless, Hinoki's greater sense of self-satisfaction seemed to be related to the promotions he had been given in the past seven years and to his overarching sense that he had been blessed throughout his life with good fortune and timing.

Hinoki spun his theory of fortune for me when I asked about his transfer from working on the line to becoming a member of a group formed in 1989 to spearhead the productivity improvement program at the factory where he worked. He said he had no special technical skills that qualified him for the new job more than other people. His superior (*uwate*) knew that Hinoki lacked that kind of experience but gave him the chance to work at it, confident that he would catch on. "In your lifetime, you probably get only three such chances," he said. I asked him how many he had had, and he answered three or four.

The first chance he had was getting hired at Yusumi. He had worked for his family's pickle business for thirteen years beforehand. At the time, the region produced many radishes and other vegetables for pickling, but the market was shrinking. He explained that pickles had been much more prominent as condiments in the prewar era, but now people were eating a lot of fried food instead. Even though business was slowing, Hinoki had intended to work with his brothers for the family business. It was then that Yusumi built a factory. Because the company needed a lot of people right away, it did not limit hiring to the latest crop of junior high or high school graduates and hired people in mid-career from other jobs. Emotionally, leaving the family business was difficult for Hinoki, but in retrospect he felt that he had been lucky. Changes were coming at a rapid pace, and he was able to ride the new wave as it overwhelmed old practices. Japan had entered its era of high-speed growth, and he had been able to take advantage

[57]

of new opportunities. He took satisfaction in seeing Japan's postwar history reflected in his own life history.

Chance had also allowed him to miraculously survive two harrowing accidents. Once, he had a head-on collision with a large truck while driving a three-wheel buggy with no doors or seat belts. He went flying through the air, lost consciousness, and woke up several days later in a hospital, with no memory of what had happened. Miraculously, he came away from the accident with only a scratch. Another time, when his buggy was loaded down with pickled vegetables, the brakes failed as he was driving down a long, steep slope leading to a sharp curve and an intersection. He tried putting a wheel into a drainage ditch alongside the road to slow himself down, but he kept gaining momentum. About 100 meters before the curve, he hit a stump protruding into the ditch. His vehicle was destroyed, but he was able to walk away, unhurt. I asked Hinoki if on both occasions he had been carrying one of the safe-driving amulets that are sold at Buddhist temples throughout Japan. He just laughed, saying that amulets had no effect other than to give the driver a little peace of mind.

Of the life "chances" Hinoki described for me, his recent promotion at Yusumi seemed somewhat different from the rest. After all, wasn't promotion based on merit? Could it be compared to his miraculous survival of accidents, or to the fortuitous coincidence of the pickling industry's decline and the opening of Yusumi's factory? I expected Hinoki, as someone who had received promotion recently, to acknowledge his own abilities and the fairness of the meritocratic system to a greater degree. Instead, he classified his promotion, along with his miraculous survival of accidents, as something over which he had no control. When I expressed disbelief, he said that he had always been honest and hardworking, but that many people were just as qualified for the promotion. How could he explain why he was chosen?

Toward the end of our second interview, Hinoki's son came home and nodded to us as he passed into the central living quarters. Hinoki told me his son worked for a sheet-metal stamping press subcontractor. He had not wanted to enter a large firm like Yusumi, where he would have been under the thumb of management much more than at a smaller firm. Hinoki understood his son's feelings and let him decide his own future. He told me the era of "chances" had largely passed with the era of high-speed growth. Fewer opportunities would present themselves now.

Promotion and Workplace Community

Hinoki's reflections on his career exemplified the ideals of Japanese workplace community described by Ronald Dore. Dore writes that the Japanese escaped the "easy-hire-fire assumption" of the labor market once they were admitted "to an enterprise community wherein benevolence, goodwill and sincerity are explicitly expected to temper the pursuit of self-interest" (Dore 1987, 183).[6] Although Hinoki spoke more of "chances" rather than benevolence, it was Yusumi that had provided him with two of these chances—a job at a critical point in the transformation of Japanese lifestyles and economy, and his recent promotion to a challenging and rewarding position. By placing these job-related chances in the same narrative as the miraculous accounts of salvation from potentially fatal traffic accidents, Hinoki portrayed Yusumi as more akin to divine providence than to a human institution of which he could make demands. While confident that he was qualified for the position to which he was promoted, he described it as a gift rather than something he could have claimed for himself.

Not all Japanese workers, however, accepted their lot as easily as did Hinoki. Firms inevitably made significant distinctions among workers, promoting certain people while holding others back, and these distinctions often led to frustration among some workers who felt that their abilities had not been recognized. Among younger workers, Masaru had outlasted 80 percent of his entering cohort, and yet felt unappreciated and planned to quit when he repaid his car loan. Among older workers, Kimata was frustrated that he had never been promoted beyond section chief. The narratives of Masaru, Kimata, and others at Yusumi show that these workers did not idealize the workplace community. If anything, the narratives depict the workplace as a "pseudo community," to use labor historian Kumazawa Makoto's term (1996, 39).

Kenichi felt much the same before he was taken off the assembly line and promoted to the maintenance section. With this promotion, he seemed much more content with himself and with his career with Yusumi. Although such promotions may not completely alleviate the ambivalence he felt about the company, he seemed on a trajectory that could lead him eventually to identify strongly with the firm as he looked back on the opportunities it had opened up for him.

To a significant degree, workers at Yusumi embraced the ideology of competitive meritocracy. Intense competition among workers for the recognition of their supervisors and promotion out of the rank and file of produc-

---

[6] Murakami and Rohlen make the similar argument that Japanese firms embed economic exchange relations within social ones. But while Dore finds the preference for community to be rooted in a Confucian heritage, Murakami and Rohlen find it to have developed in the historical circumstances of the early postwar period (Murakami and Rohlen 1992, 90) and predict that this preference will change as pressures to open domestic markets and to compete with low-wage-labor Asian economies make more flexible economic exchange relations within Japan inevitable (ibid., 104).

tion workers has destroyed community defined in terms of solidarity among workers (see Kumazawa 1996, 67). Those few who were successful in the competition for promotion downplayed their claim to recognition, transferring it into an embrace of the firm as a benevolent community. Their identification with the community of the firm was not shared by the many workers who were passed over for promotion. These workers were left with ambivalent feelings, not unlike workers in smaller, less prestigious manufacturing firms (see Roberson 1998, Kondo 1990).

In certain contexts, however, the presence of foreign workers has prompted some Japanese workers to emphasize what they had felt to be lacking at Yusumi—a strong sense of community—as a distinguishing characteristic of Japanese workplaces which Nikkeijin and other foreign workers supposedly could not appreciate.

Windbreakers and the Discourse on Workplace Culture

At the end of their stint at Yusumi, all foreign trainees were given a windbreaker with the company logo written boldly across the back. A few days before they were to leave, several Chinese trainees went from door to door in the dormitory, trying to sell their windbreakers to the Japanese and non-Chinese foreign workers for five thousand yen (roughly $50)—half off the official retail price in the company store. The dormitory supervisors were upset when they heard about this. They expected the gifts from Yusumi to stimulate a sense of obligation in the trainees. Instead, the Chinese appeared to reject the meaning of these gifts. The Japanese supervisors were unable to understand the reaction of the Chinese trainees, for whom five thousand yen was almost equal to a month's wages in China. Economic exchange is often presented in the form of social exchange (Rohlen and Murakami 1992, Appadurai 1986), yet the dormitory supervisors saw only the social aspect of their relationship with Chinese trainees and were appalled when the Chinese exposed hardheaded economics that lay just beneath the surface.

The economic relationship between trainees and Yusumi was fairly effectively hidden by the way that management defined these workers as trainees, and by the fact that it took care of all aspects of these workers' lives in Japan. Transportation, housing, food, and an occasional excursion were all paid for by Yusumi. The relationship between Yusumi and its trainees appeared to be charitable. In addition, the paternalistic injunctions of Japanese law stipulated that the function of the trainee system was to contribute to international cooperation through the transfer of technology and thereby to help develop human capital and social and economic conditions in foreign countries (Tezuka 1995, 64–5). The actual program as realized by Yusumi, however, had greater economic benefit for Yusumi than it did for the trainees or the countries they came from. The Japanese government had stipulated that trainee programs should provide technical or Japanese language training for at least one third of the time during the training period, the rest of which could be devoted to on-the-job training. In reality, Yusumi management had its trainees working on the line for almost their entire stint. The only training the company provided was just one week of language instruction. Management nevertheless took advantage of the trainee program to pay these workers a stipend far below formal workers' minimum wages. In contrast to the roughly 230,000 yen per month ($2,300) made by contract workers (Nikkeijin and Japanese alike) at Yusumi, Korean trainees earned 90,000 yen per month, plus another 25,000 from their employer in Korea. This was a somewhat better deal than that of the Indian trainees, who earned 80,000 per month, and Chinese, who earned only 50,000. The differential wages were based in part on the differences in the standards of living and exchange rates between Japan and these countries.

Nikkeijin were similarly criticized as lacking a sense of responsibility *(sekinin kan)* toward the firms for which they worked, jumping from job to job for even the slightest increase in wages. Such criticisms came not only from Japanese workers but also from bureaucrats, academics, and managers. Japanese managers interviewed by sociologist Watanabe Masako portrayed employer-employee relations among Japanese as infused by a peculiar Japanese-style feeling and consideration *(nihon teki hairyo)*. According to these managers, Nikkeijin upset the reciprocal obligations between Japanese managers and Japanese workers. One manager complained that Nikkeijin often quit without notice and lacked a sense of gratitude for all he had provided for them (Watanabe 1995, 81). Other Japanese managers had a variety of complaints:

- They (Nikkeijin) don't come on time.
- They don't keep their promises.
- Even if they do what they are told, they never take the initiative to do something on their own.
- They don't have the consideration to do things so other people can do their tasks more easily.
- They don't think in terms of the group's responsibility.
- When they are starting out, they can't do as much work as others, but when they are eventually given more work than initially, they complain and say that their pay should rise as well.
- Even though you've worked with them a while and taught them a lot,

[61]

they'll quit in an instant if a good paying job comes up, or if there's something that bugs them.
• They make strong demands for overtime work. (Ibid., 82)

The Japanese discourse on foreign workers ignored the significant turnover among younger Japanese workers, as well as the ambivalence of many Japanese workers toward their firms.

Despite frustrations and ambivalence among Japanese workers, the presence of foreign workers motivated some Japanese workers to draw on the discourse about "Japanese rules," responsibility *(sekinin sei)*, and reciprocal bonds so frequently used by managers, academics, and local government officials, as a means of buttressing their sense of self-worth. John Lie makes a similar point in his analysis of the debate among Japanese intellectuals over foreign workers. He writes: "The reality of multiethnicity once again threatened and affirmed the belief in monoethnicity. Precisely when multiethnicity became incontrovertible, people asserted that Japan has been, always and already, monoethnic" (Lie 2001, 26). In addition to ethnic homogeneity, I would argue that the presence of foreign workers revived assumptions of cultural homogeneity based on supposedly traditional workplace practices.

A number of practices were established at Yusumi to ensure that distinct lines between Japanese and foreign were maintained. Nikkeijin were generally segregated in different dormitories. Nikkeijin and foreign trainees who shared the same dormitory with Japanese were segregated in the bathing arrangement. Within the factory, foreign workers were marked by their yellow hats. In addition, workers for the in-house subcontractors, the vast majority of whom were Nikkeijin, all wore different uniforms from those of Yusumi workers and were physically marginalized on the peripheries of the factory. Tensions and discontent arose where the lines between these groups were blurred, as in the case of Nikkeijin salaries that rivaled those of younger Japanese workers. Although Japanese firms originally recruited Nikkeijin as an alternative to other foreign workers because Nikkeijin had been depicted in various contexts as essentially Japanese, Japanese workers were threatened by Nikkeijin boundary crossing. The attitudes of Yusumi managers toward Nikkeijin also seemed to shift as the managers found foreign trainees to be a much cheaper source of labor.

To better understand some of these dynamics, we should regard culture as a toolbox of resilient symbolic resources that can be deployed for rhetorical or political purposes at appropriate moments (see di Leonardo 1984), rather than as a fixed structure of thought or behavior that can be discerned in all members of a culture in all contexts. Japanese could draw on certain resources to construct differences and to maintain boundaries between themselves and Nikkeijin when they felt that it was in their interest to do so.

These resources could be harnessed to build solidarity between Japanese and foreign workers just as well as to build barriers. Such a possibility existed at Yusumi, even if it was not realized. Although many Japanese workers were critical of Nikkeijin and other foreign workers, few were overtly antagonistic toward them. Kenichi actually took an active interest in foreign workers and had learned several Korean words and phrases. Both Kimata and Masaru got along well with the foreign workers they supervised. The possibility of understanding and solidarity between Japanese workers (as opposed to managers) and Nikkeijin is explored further in chapter 6. In the next chapter, I explore some of the consequences of the negative stereotypes of Nikkeijin—the legitimization of employment practices that marginalized them in workplace communities, restricted their access to health care, and limited their compensation in cases of workplace accidents.

[4]

Accidents, Apologies, and Compensation

The majority of Nikkeijin in Hamamatsu worked for subcontractors that supplied parts to larger, reputable firms such as Yusumi. The conditions in these smaller firms were more varied than they were in the larger ones. Although Nikkeijin were marginalized within Yusumi, they nevertheless enjoyed both health insurance and accident insurance. There was a conscious effort at Yusumi to make the workplace a safe environment. During the months I worked there, I met only one person who had suffered an injury other than a repetitive-stress injury common among line workers. An electronic sign at the factory gates kept count of the number of recorded accidents that had occurred at the factory over the past year. Never exceeding more than four or five, it advertised Yusumi's commitment to safety.

Safety standards regulated all Japanese workplaces, but some firms gave safety greater emphasis than others. The difference in conditions among firms was inscribed on the bodies of many Nikkeijin who worked at subcontracting firms through employment brokers. Women who soldered circuit boards often developed rashes on their faces because of poor ventilation. Others who used microscopes complained that their vision was no longer as sharp as it had been. One friend of mine was hospitalized along with several of his Japanese coworkers because of a toxic gas leak. The loss of fingers in metal stamping presses was the most common of the serious injuries I encountered among Nikkeijin. Occasionally a newspaper reported that a Nikkeijin had died in a workplace accident. I decided to conduct formal interviews with people who had been injured in workplace accidents, to find out why accidents were so common, how people dealt with the trauma of injury, and what kind of compensation they received.

Accidents provided a particularly dramatic context in which to examine how membership within workplace communities was negotiated between workers and their managers. What level of risk were workers willing to live with and what kind of compensation did they expect when they were injured? A higher rate of reconciliation between Japanese workers and their managers suggests a certain cultural attitude with regard to the importance of community. The higher rate of rupture between Nikkeijin workers and their managers suggests a cultural attitude that emphasized self-interest. However, a closer look at the narratives of injured workers suggests another interpretation—one that points to the impact of the structural marginalization of Nikkeijin within the employment system. Smaller firms generally used employment brokers, which marked Nikkeijin as outsiders. Managers of these firms did not feel as much responsibility toward brokered workers as they did to their full-time workers, and this often translated into uncaring treatment of injured Nikkeijin workers. A study of the interaction between workers and managers after accidents illustrates that the employment status of workers was more significant than their cultural background in determining whether the incident ended in amicable reconciliation or antagonistic rupture.

Surprisingly, the narratives of injured Nikkeijin indicate that most would have been willing to reconcile with their managers after accidents, and that it was the treatment they received that motivated them to demand that their managers acknowledge responsibility for the accidents more formally and compensate them financially. The marginalization of Nikkeijin in the employment system led to interactions that exacerbated relations between them and their Japanese managers. Furthermore, the informal employment system for Nikkeijin in Hamamatsu not only denied them a feeling of belonging within workplaces; it also often denied them basic protections mandated by law such as health insurance and accident insurance.

Employment Brokers

The employment system for Nikkeijin in Hamamatsu was dominated by employment brokers throughout in the 1990s. Such brokers had handled seasonal Japanese workers from other parts of the country during the postwar period of high-speed economic growth, but the numbers of such workers had diminished significantly by the 1980s. The influx of Nikkeijin in the late 1980s led to a renewed proliferation of brokers, who established as many as 150 employment agencies (*assen gaisha* in Japanese; *empreteira* in Portuguese) in the Hamamatsu region alone in the early 1990s.

In the late 1980s and early 1990s, brokers recruited workers from Brazil.

[65]

Japanese brokers worked with Nikkeijin-run travel agencies in Brazil to provide prospective migrants with round-trip tickets (see Bornstein 1992). Migrants paid for these tickets in installments when they arrived in Japan and started working at jobs procured by the broker. A certain amount was deducted from their paychecks every month until their loans had been repaid. Because international labor recruitment targeting a specific ethnic group was not permitted by the International Labor Organization, much of the advertisement was done in the Japanese language press, in Brazil through word of mouth, and by other informal means. By the early 1990s, brokers had started to recruit workers from the ballooning number of Nikkeijin already in Japan. Job ads placed by employment brokers filled several pages in each of the Portuguese language newspapers in Japan every week.

In addition to recruiting workers, brokers had to establish relationships with firms interested in a Nikkeijin workforce. Some brokers were small operations and supplied a handful of workers to just one firm. Other brokers cultivated relationships with multiple firms and dealt with as many as five hundred Nikkeijin workers. In the mid-1990s, manufacturing firms often paid brokers 1,800 yen (roughly $18 at the time) per hour for male workers and 1,400 yen per hour for female workers. Brokers would generally keep about 30 percent of these receipts for themselves, setting male workers' wages at 1,300 yen per hour and female wages at 900 yen per hour.

Many small manufacturers and other businesses used brokers because they did not have the means to recruit Nikkeijin on their own. In addition, brokers provided a variety of services necessary to maintain these workers. Brokers arranged to rent apartments from landlords, to help fill out documents necessary to renew visas, and to look after a multitude of issues that migrants faced in adjusting to work and life in Japan. In order to meet the needs of the workers, brokers generally had on staff at least one Nikkeijin who was conversant in both Japanese and Portuguese. Mirella Shimizu had worked for a broker for about a year and a half when I interviewed her. When she first arrived in Japan, she had worked in a factory. Her garrulous and personable style attracted the attention of her broker, who persuaded her to work in his office. She described her varied duties there:

> I was an interpreter. . . . I did translations. I was a driver. I was a telephone operator. I cleaned up around the office. . . . I did everything. I'd go to the immigration office with Brazilians to take care of visa paperwork. I would go to city hall with them, to the alien registration desk. I did almost all of that for our office.

When I interviewed her, she was thinking of giving up her office job and moving back to the factory. Factory work was less stressful, she said. She described some of the problems that routinely came up in her work, often involving other Nikkeijin who made demands on her that she was not in a position to meet:

Brazilians make for a lot of work. They would call me: "Mirella!! This is crap! What a pain! (*Essa porcaria! Que puxa vida!*) I want some pots and pans! I want a TV! I want a cleaner room! You get it? The salary here is low! I want my pay earlier!" There were people who were respectful, who would ask me, "Mirella, I'm sorry, but could you do me a favor? Is there something you can do?" And I like doing favors. But there were others who'd come to me— "Mirella! Porcaria!" You know what I mean? These people only complain. And moreover, they say things like "You don't help us at all. You're a brownnoser. You brownnose, and you make good money." This is what they believe; just because I dressed in a skirt, because I'd be in clean clothes, they'd think that I was earning real well. It wasn't true. I was earning better than I did in the factory. But I had a lot to do all the time. And long hours. I couldn't go home at six. I'd have to stay on till seven or eight every day. And I'd have to get up early to start work. I'd have to work every Saturday as well. It was tiring. But logically, since this agency has a lot of workers here in Hamamatsu, I believe there are more than 150 workers, and for every ten people, there are one or two jerks (*chatos*). These people, I tell you. . . . You know those two, the guy with the beard (referring to a couple she had greeted politely at a Brazilian grocery a few minutes earlier)? That couple gave me a headache. They'd be calling me with complaints. . . . If it was something I could do, I'd do it. It is just that I can't do things on my own. When someone asks me if I could do something for them, I'd tell them to wait while I asked the boss, and if he says yes, I'd do it. If he says no, I'd go back to the worker and tell him I'm sorry but I can't do this. It's just that at times, the person doesn't understand this side. He thinks that I'm the one that's the problem, that I just don't feel like doing the favor. And there are so many people asking for favors, and I'm just one person.

Mirella played a crucial role at her employment agency, as mediator between workers, managers, and brokers. It was an extremely taxing position, one that led her to pointed criticisms of the Brazilians she worked with. She recognized that some of them had legitimate grievances, but could not sympathize with others' sense of entitlement.

Not all brokers were so critical of their Nikkeijin employees. Several thought that they were excellent workers, especially when they came to Japan with the intention of saving money to send home to buy a house, start a business, or help their families in other ways. One of the brokers praised Nikkeijin, saying, "They come to Japan for a purpose, and they don't waste money" (*muda tsukai wa shinai*). One Nikkeijin who started her own agency admitted that several of her workers were difficult to handle, but added that she screened most troublemakers out in the hiring process. She noted that many of her workers had been with her for four or five years, and one had been there for eight years; she said these veterans helped teach the newer recruits about her expectations. The average tenure at her agency appeared considerably longer than at some of the Japanese-run agencies, where people often left after only six months.

Many brokers were responsive to the needs of their Nikkeijin workers, even when the brokers were at times frustrated by their demands. Despite the goodwill of individual brokers or manufacturers, however, the employment system as a whole functioned to marginalize Nikkeijin. Most Hamamatsu firms that employed foreigners filled less than 15 percent of jobs with foreign workers (Kitagawa 1993, 185–86). One manager said he viewed foreign workers as a cushion to use in riding over bumpy economic fluctuations. Keeping foreign workers to between 5 and 10 percent of the workforce allowed the firm just the right amount of flexibility required to respond to economic cycles. Foreign workers hired through employment brokers could be laid off with little notice. During hard times, larger firms that guaranteed their workers permanent employment sometimes transferred them to subcontractors, who would make way for them by laying off their brokered workers. About two hundred Nikkeijin were laid off in 1993 for this reason in one well publicized case in the city of Kosai, just west of Hamamatsu. The Kosai layoff made local and national news because of the large number of workers involved (*Mainichi Shimbun*, October 15, 1993; *Shizuoka Shimbun*, October 16, 1993; *Chūnichi Shimbun*, March 11, 1994), but during recessions, numerous such incidents occurred, albeit usually on a smaller scale (Monna November 1993, October 1995). Brokered workers were on the margins of a Japanese employment system that remained centered on the ideal, if not the reality, of lifetime employment and seniority wages.

The unsupervised system of employment brokers that dominated the labor market for Nikkeijin in Hamamatsu also allowed for a significant amount of discrimination and exploitation. The Japanese language press carried stories of evil employment agencies (*akushitsu assen gaisha*) that skimmed off a large percentage of their workers' salaries or overcharged for various services, sometimes confiscating their workers' passports until the loans for their exorbitant airline tickets had been paid in full.[1] In lieu of any effective government system overseeing migration and employment, however, employment agencies provided crucial services for both manufacturers and migrants.

---

[1] Brokers often charged as much as 350,000 yen ($3,500) for a round-trip ticket that they could acquire for only 100,000 yen. The loans they provided Nikkeijin, although tied to the sale of exorbitant airline tickets, made migration possible for many who otherwise would not have been able to raise money on their own for their tickets.

Aside from providing manufacturing firms the means to recruit and to maintain a Nikkeijin labor force, the system of employment brokers also relieved manufacturing firms of the legal obligations of employers toward their employees. The most onerous and significant such obligation was the provision of health insurance. Almost all Japanese employees were covered either by the government-sponsored employee health insurance (*shakai hoken*) or by policies offered by officially recognized health insurance cooperatives. Few Nikkeijin employees were covered by these forms of insurance.

Although many young, single migrants were not interested in costly insurance, those who were raising families in Japan searched for jobs that would provide insurance or moved to cities whose governments would enroll them in national health insurance. In comparison with other migrant groups, Nikkeijin men and women had come to Japan in relatively balanced numbers, and a considerable number of workers had school-aged children or were planning families in Japan. Such was the case with Sueli Takano, a Nikkeijin friend who was pregnant in Japan when I finished the bulk of my fieldwork in 1996.

I went back to Hamamatsu in the summer of 1997 and visited Sueli in a public-housing project by Hamamatsu's famous sand dunes facing the ocean. The new apartment was much more spacious and airy than the one she and her husband had rented from his employment broker the previous year. Her pregnancy had been difficult, and I imagined that the medical bills must have been high because of the complications. Her husband's broker did not provide health insurance, and I wondered how she had managed to pay her bills.

> Sueli: I had this problem of toxemia [blood poisoning]. . . . I was very bloated, with very high arterial pressure. . . . But I was treated very well at Seirei Hospital. The doctors there treated me very well; they received me, gave me medicine, and my pressure started to normalize.
>
> JR: This was already the eighth month?
>
> Sueli: Eighth month. But Julia [her baby] had already stopped growing the previous month, the seventh. And the placenta, in the fourth month [stopped growing]. A small placenta, a small baby. With little amniotic liquid. We were in a difficult situation—the baby could have been born with pulmonary problems or any other kind of problem. When I went to the hospital, they helped me a lot; they helped me get health insurance. The hospital was able to apply some pressure and get me health insurance; they were able to do various things for me. . . . I didn't have the means to pay, for it was very expensive. Without insurance, it would have been 3 million yen.[2]

---

[2] At the exchange rate of 100 yen to the dollar, this would have amounted to $30,000.

I was surprised that Sueli was able to get employee insurance, for most brokers defied the requirement to provide health insurance with impunity. Sueli explained:

> We asked for it once when I was interned, and they [the employment brokers] said no. We asked a second time and they said no. The third time, it was the hospital that asked. And they [the brokers] accepted it. . . . The administrative section of the hospital asked me for the telephone number and address of the brokers, the people's names.

Several months later, Sueli's husband, Leonardo, got a job at a firm much closer to the public housing into which they had recently moved. Sueli explained that Leonardo's employment agency gave them some trouble when he turned in his resignation:

> They said that since they had provided him with shakai hoken when I was in the hospital, he had to give them back the money they had paid the government for our insurance (laughs). They wanted something like 360,000 yen [$3,600] or so. So they didn't issue the last paycheck, worth something like 400,000 yen. . . . We went to the Ministry of Labor, (laughs) the *rōdō kantokusho* [Labor Standards Inspection Office]. And they called the brokers, and they (the brokers) said, *"Wa, sonna koto nai desu. Tori ni kite kudasai."* ["It's nothing like that. Come by and pick up the paycheck."]

Sueli had lived in Japan seven years at the time, she could speak Japanese relatively well, and she was informed about her rights and about where she could go for help. Even for her, however, it was only through a great deal of persistence and help from the hospital staff and the Labor Standards Inspection Office (LSIO) that she was able first to obtain health insurance to cover her pregnancy and later to receive her husband's final paycheck.

Not only were most Nikkeijin denied health insurance; some who worked through brokers also had difficulty getting compensation after being injured in workplace accidents. Brokers often avoided enrolling their workers in mandatory accident insurance. When workers were injured in accidents, the local nonprofit organization looking after the interests of foreign workers was able to put pressure on some brokers to enroll injured workers after the fact. But many injured workers, not knowing where to turn, ended up returning to Brazil to recuperate before filing the necessary forms with the LSIO in order to receive compensation. And in some cases of workplace accidents, the understaffing of the LSIO often made it difficult for this agency to resolve problems that Nikkeijin encountered with their managers and brokers.

Sueli received help from the LSIO in pressuring the broker to pay her husband's final paycheck. She also benefited from the government-sponsored low-income housing. The benefits that Japanese government agencies provided to Nikkeijin have led Takeyuki Tsuda to suggest:

> Institutional discrimination is not a problem, and in fact, some Japanese institutions openly welcome the Japanese-Brazilians. . . . Local governments have also been institutionally receptive to the Japanese-Brazilians, allowing them to fully participate and benefit from local government service such as Japanese language classes and health insurance programs. (Tsuda 1998, 349)

Not all government agencies were so helpful, however. With regard to the issue of health insurance, the Ministry of Health and Welfare (*Kōseishō*) and the Hamamatsu city government helped establish and maintain a system of institutional discrimination.

Bureaucrats, Brazilians, and Health Insurance

The difficulty that Sueli's husband had with his employment agency was not unusual. Almost all Nikkeijin in Japan were employed, but few had employee health insurance. The Ministry of Health and Welfare, which administrated the employee health insurance program, had no power to enforce the law requiring firms to provide insurance to their employees. And the Hamamatsu city government was reluctant to crack down on employment brokers because of the central role they played in recruiting Nikkeijin. This was the case even though the Employment Security Law (*Shokugyō antei hō*) recognized the operation of employment brokers in only fifteen occupations, none of which included unskilled factory work—the kind of work most Nikkeijin were engaged in. The quasi-legal status of employment brokers for Nikkeijin invited the entry of local gangsters (*yakuza*), who thought little of the legal obligations of employers. Even the relatively honest brokers, however, avoided providing health insurance.

Unable to get insurance through their workplace, many Nikkeijin went to city hall to apply for national health insurance. The National Health Insurance and Pensions Act, passed in 1959 to cover all "self-employed individuals, farmers, retired people, and their dependents," provided coverage for roughly 30 percent of the Japanese population by 1986 (Powell and Anesaki 1990, 130–32). National health insurance (*kokumin kenkō hoken*) was first

[71]

made available to foreigners in 1986 after a long struggle for access by second- and third-generation permanent resident Koreans who did not hold Japanese citizenship *(Zainichi kankokujin)* (Miyajima and Higuchi 1996, 21). Surprisingly, prior to 1994, the majority of Nikkeijin in Hamamatsu were enrolled in national health insurance. In April of that year, however, the Ministry of Health and Welfare issued an internal memo to local governments pressuring them not to accept foreign workers' applications for national health insurance; the memo urged the governments to advise workers to get employee insurance through their firms (Monna 1994).[3] Since then, almost all Nikkeijin who have gone to city hall to apply for health insurance have been turned away with the explanation that if they were unemployed or self-employed they would be eligible, but since they had employers, they had to get insurance through those firms, which were legally required to offer it. Meanwhile, the cities of Toyota in Aichi Prefecture, Kawasaki in Kanagawa Prefecture, and Ōta in Gumma Prefecture, along with some other cities with high concentrations of Nikkeijin, continued for at least several more years to make national health insurance available for brokered workers.

Grupo Justiça e Paz, a volunteer organization formed for the purpose of pressuring the Hamamatsu city government on the health insurance issue, drafted a letter in the summer of 1997 claiming that only 13 percent of Brazilians[4] in Hamamatsu had any form of health insurance. My own research, based on hospital records, indicates that between 20 percent and 30 percent of Brazilians in Hamamatsu had some form of insurance, fairly close to the 30 percent figure another volunteer group, Medical Aid for Foreigners, found in a survey of 340 foreigners who received free medical exams on October 19, 1997.

In response to the claims of these volunteer groups, city bureaucrats I spoke to pointed to the results of a survey they had commissioned the previous year. The survey found that more that 60 percent of Brazilians had some form of health insurance and that most of them had one of the two kinds mandated by Japanese law (Hamamatsu-shi kokusai kōryū shitsu 1997, 8). During a meeting of the city council called to address the health care issue, city politicians defended their decision not to accept applications for na-

[3] Officials in the Ministry of Health and Welfare were no doubt motivated to write the memo out of budgetary concerns; government subsidies for national health insurance amounted to 45 percent of benefits paid plus administrative costs, considerably more than subsidies to employee insurance programs, which were less than 10 percent of expenditures (Powell and Anesaki 1990, 137).

[4] I use the term "Brazilian" here rather than "Nikkeijin" to follow the usage of these studies. "Brazilian" includes mestizos and non-Nikkeijin spouses and therefore is more accurate when referring to the overall migrant community from Brazil.

tional health insurance. They rested their case on the authority of Japanese law, arguing that national health insurance was for those who were not employed in firms. The Japanese newspaper *Shizuoka Shimbun* reported that one assemblyman shouted in frustration to continued questioning that if Brazilians were not satisfied, they should return home (May 24, 1997). The story was carried the next day in the Portuguese language newspaper *Nova Visão* (May 25, 1997). The assemblyman was taken to task in both the Japanese and Portuguese language media, but for some Japanese I spoke to, it was his indiscretion more than his sentiment that was deplorable. *Decorum*

Another city bureaucrat I interviewed claimed that most Brazilians had health insurance, and that those who did not were opportunists who did not like the idea of paying premiums while they were healthy. To this bureaucrat, Sueli's last-minute decision to apply for insurance when she confronted a medical emergency would exemplify Brazilians' abuse of the insurance system. He also speculated that health insurance may not exist in Brazil and that Brazilians may not even understand the concept of insurance.

I knew many Brazilians who did not want to pay the insurance premiums, but their reasons contrasted sharply with this bureaucrat's speculation. Japanese as well as Brazilians complained about the cost of insurance. Brazilians, however, had greater reason to complain since national health insurance in Hamamatsu, as in most of Japan, came bundled with a pension program—and the premiums for the latter doubled those for health insurance. Previously in Hamamatsu, Brazilians had been able to receive health insurance without having to simultaneously enroll in the pension program, but this changed in 1994. Although the national government encouraged this bundling and actually mandated it in the case of its employee insurance programs, local governments have had the option to administer it in different ways. In 1994, the Hamamatsu city government caved in to pressure from the national Ministry of Health and Welfare and required the bundling of the insurance and pension programs.

In order to receive benefits from the pension program, a person had to pay into it for a minimum of twenty years, far longer than almost any Brazilian planned to stay in Japan. The bundling of the pension and health insurance programs, plus the minimum year requirement to receive benefits from the pension program, meant that even if Nikkeijin had been allowed to continue to enroll for national insurance, the majority who were single and healthy would not have been interested in doing so.[5] Since April 1996, foreigners leaving Japan have become eligible for a partial refund of the

[5] David McConnell (2000, 71–73) describes the angry response of Americans and other foreign English teachers hired through the Japan Exchange and Teaching (JET) program when they were required to pay toward pension programs from which they would never receive benefits.

first three years of payments they made into the pension program. This has only partially resolved the problem for the many Brazilians who have been working in Japan, however. The Hamamatsu city bureaucrat I spoke to interpreted Brazilian actions as irresponsible, as if the Brazilians could have enrolled for insurance if they had wanted to. Insurance was not made available for most Nikkeijin, however, and even if it had been, their reluctance to pay for a pension program they would never benefit from was understandable.

When I asked another city bureaucrat about the dilemma that Nikkeijin faced—being turned away by city hall for national health insurance and being denied employee health insurance by their brokers—I was given another set of statistics that dismissed the gravity of the issue. According to annual surveys done by the Ministry of Labor's Employment Security Office (*Shokugyō Anteisho*) in Hamamatsu, the majority of Brazilians were hired directly by firms rather than through brokers. My own research produced very different numbers. The vast majority of Brazilians I had met over two years in Hamamatsu were brokered. Those who were not tended to be concentrated in the larger, more established manufacturers. I have calculated that 75 percent of foreign workers were hired through brokers. Activist Monna Kunio of the Hamamatsu Overseas Laborers Solidarity (HLS) estimated the figure to be closer to 90 percent (Monna March 1993, 58–63). The low figures produced in the Employment Security Office surveys probably reflected manufacturing firms' fear of admitting use of illegally brokered workers. Manufacturing firms generally claimed that they used subcontractors rather than brokers, and brokers themselves tried to pass themselves off as subcontractors.

Instead of arguing over the data, I asked the bureaucrat to imagine the dilemma of Nikkeijin hired through brokers. In lieu of an alternative, could not the city cover such workers through national health insurance? He replied that city hall could only follow the law, which stipulated that salaried workers should get employee insurance rather than national health insurance. I argued that the National Health Insurance and Pensions Act of 1959 was designed precisely to cover those who did not have insurance through their employers. Since Nikkeijin in effect did not have access to employee insurance, did not city hall have the responsibility to cover them? He replied that certain laws had precedence over others.

Much like the European national bureaucrats whose rhetoric Michael Herzfeld has analyzed, Japanese bureaucrats, in response to foreign workers' requests for access to health insurance, claimed that they could only act neutrally, and in accordance with law. They claimed the law as a unitary and self-evident authority, to mask "a host of legalistic interpretations at various levels of administrative differentiation" (Herzfeld 1992, 93). In fact, it was just one interpretation of two conflicting laws that led to Brazilian exclusion from health insurance. Japanese bureaucrats reinforced their self-image as neutral and rational through the production of vast quantities of data, which had the aura of scientific and impartial truth.

The production of such forms of knowledge, which in Japan has often involved the close collaboration of academic social scientists, was far from neutral. Among Hamamatsu businesses, employment brokers fostered a dependency on brokered foreign workers. The city government turned a blind eye and allowed these brokers to operate beyond the pale of certain legal codes, and may even have colluded with these agencies. One former broker told me that city officials were quietly advising brokers on how to pass themselves off as subcontractors when filing their tax returns.

The lack of effort to enforce labor regulations regarding the employment system for Nikkeijin had a significant impact on their lives in Hamamatsu. People whose medical conditions could have been treated effectively at an early stage often avoided professional care until their conditions became much more serious. The stereotype of Nikkeijin self-interest helped the bureaucracy, managers, and academics justify the marginal position of Nikkeijin in the employment system. Although some Nikkeijin were happy with an employment system that made it relatively easy for them to pick and choose among workplaces, others desired greater stability and security. Such security was hard to come by, however, in a context in which employment brokers dominated the labor market for Nikkeijin.

Workplace Accidents

At first glance, stereotypes of Nikkeijin self-interest and Japanese group orientation appear to bear themselves out in the aftermath of workplace accidents. Many Japanese workers returned to work after recovering from their injuries without demanding compensation beyond indemnities from accident insurance. Nikkeijin often left their firms on bad terms with management. The following cases, however, suggest that Nikkeijin were often driven to pursue justice in the legal realm only after their desires for reconciliation and amicable relations within the workplace community were frustrated, often as a result of their status as brokered workers. They did not desire membership in a community characterized by unquestioned loyalty, however, where individual injuries were considered necessary sacrifices for the larger good (a kind of community that was not uncommon in early postwar Japanese workplaces). Rather, they envisioned a community where superiors earned loyalty through the reciprocal provision of benevolence and care. It was only when managers excluded Nikkeijin workers from membership in a just community—a community defined through reciprocal relationships—that these workers sought justice in the courts.[6]

Vanessa Kimura

Vanessa was only sixteen years old when I interviewed her. She had lost half of the middle finger and ring finger on her right hand a year earlier and was trying to take the owner of the firm to court. Tall and slender, she was an aspiring model, and participated in fashion shows in Hamamatsu at a Brazilian culture center (see chapter 5). She was animated and self-assured during our interview. Rather than breaking her spirit, her horrible experience seemed to have fostered in her a maturity unusual in someone her age. As a third generation Nikkeijin, she spoke little Japanese before going to Japan. She noted that her Japanese language ability had gotten much better in the year since the accident, because she had had to talk so often with lawyers, doctors, and labor standards bureaucrats.

Only four other people worked at the factory where Vanessa had been injured: the Japanese manager and his wife, Vanessa's mother, and a young Nikkeijin man. Vanessa's mother had been concerned about having her fifteen-year-old daughter work at the presses. When a position opened up, however, Vanessa's mother decided that it would be good for them both to have jobs in the same place. Her boss reassured her that it was safe and that he would look after her daughter.

Vanessa described her boss as always hurried and sloppy in his work. He had spent his entire working life at the presses. One day, frustrated with the Nikkeijin man for not working faster, the boss had Vanessa take his place. It was Vanessa's first time to work at that press, and she did not know whether the safety sensor was functioning or turned on. Her Japanese was not very good at that time and her boss did not bother to have anyone properly explain how to use the press.

The accident happened shortly before lunch break. Vanessa was hungry and was thinking about what she was going to eat. She did not feel or notice anything, and just grabbed for the next metal part to insert into the press. When she was unable to pick it up, she looked at what she was doing, but still did not notice her tattered glove. Then she looked back at the press and noticed part of a finger with bone exposed dangling from the upper block.

---

[6] See Thomas C. Smith (1988) for an illuminating discussion of how Japanese industrial workers in the Meiji era framed their protests about working conditions in terms of benevolence rather than in terms of more universal rights.

Mute, she held her now bleeding hand in front of her. Her boss had been working at a press directly opposite her, she said, but he just stared at her in astonishment, until her mother came over and started screaming the name of God, and someone called an ambulance. Vanessa's voice was strained with emotion as she forced herself to recount these details. She did not feel any pain immediately after the accident, and she stood there thinking about how she might have lost her entire hand; she also thought about how young she was, how beautiful her boyfriend was, how she wanted to be a model, and how maybe now she would not be able to realize her dreams.

After the accident, her boss appeared remorseful and assured her that accident insurance would cover her wages while she was recovering; he said she would receive an indemnity as well. But after a couple of weeks, he suggested that she might forfeit her insurance compensation if she did not return to work soon. Three weeks after the accident, with much trepidation, Vanessa returned to one of the presses and started work anew. Being back was horrible, because she relived the accident with every moment. She worked very slowly and deliberately. Her boss soon lost patience and started shouting at her to work faster. Possibly fearing that another accident might disfigure her remaining good hand, she continued to use her injured right hand, picking up the metal pieces with just her thumb and forefinger. This provoked her boss, who came over, grabbed her left wrist, and shouted, "Use your good hand! Use your good hand!"

It was this treatment that motivated her to sue, Vanessa said. "How could he speak to me like that, considering it was his fault I had gotten injured?" She added:

> I don't think that I'm an animal, Joshua. I'm human; I'm very human. . . . I have Japanese blood in me—my grandmother is Japanese. Understand? I think he should have treated me as a human, for I'm not an animal. I don't know whether it's because Japanese are real cold, in relation to sentiments, but when it comes to money . . . they're going to die for money.

Vanessa was outraged at being treated like "an animal," in a way that nullified her humanity. Her boss failed to indicate a sincere sense of remorse or sympathy—the minimum standards of human behavior as Vanessa understood it. Her boss's obsession with profits and productivity eclipsed any sympathy he may have had for her. Vanessa's narrative suggested that apologies, gestures of care (hospital visits, inquiries about her well-being), and expressions of condolence (collection of sympathy money from all employees and managers), combined with financial compensation from accident insurance, may have been sufficient to bring about a reconciliation between

[77]

her and the firm. More than anything else, however, it was the manager's lack of sympathy and remorse that motivated Vanessa to pursue retributive justice in the legal system.

Even as Vanessa resolved to find justice in the legal system, she clung to the ideal of community. "I have Japanese blood in me," she said, appealing to her membership within an ethnically defined community in the same breath in which she emphasized her humanity—"I don't think that I'm an animal. . . . I'm very human. . . ." She expressed indignation that her Japanese ancestry had no effect on her boss's attitude. Why did it not guaranteed her membership within the community of the Japanese workplace? Vanessa's statement indicates that the particularistic community of a firm, a race, or a nation is not necessarily in conflict with the universalistic sense of common humanity. Rather, particularistic communities could be created by acknowledging common humanity through reciprocal acts of respect and care. Given what she interpreted to be her exclusion from the community, the legal system could satisfy Vanessa in two respects. First, it could act as a higher authority to confirm her humanity. Second, it could provide her with the satisfaction of retributive justice against someone who had denied her humanity and excluded her from a just community. Even as she moved closer to the position of the liberal citizen intent on realizing her individual rights to financial compensation and punitive damages, Vanessa's narrative and metaphors continued to justify her actions in terms of denial of community.

Community of Destiny

Reported workplace accidents have declined substantially since the establishment of labor standards in the postwar period. Between 1965 and 1990, they fell nearly 50 percent, from 408,331 to 210,108 (Hōsei Daigaku Ōhara Shakai Mondai Kenkyūsho 1992, 96).[7] In all likelihood, however, accidents and injuries have always been underreported. When Nikkeijin were injured, brokers often paid their medical bills in cash and thereby avoid reporting the circumstances of the accident. A record of accidents could lead to more thorough and frequent visits by labor standards inspectors. One

---

[7] The accidents recorded in 1965 included only those that resulted in workers missing eight or more days of work. In 1973, the survey redefined serious injury as anything that led to four or more days' absence from work. The more inclusive definition indicates that the reduction in accidents from 1965 to 1990 was even greater than the statistics indicate. In addition, the number of deaths declined by 58 percent, from 6,046 in 1965 to 2,550 in 1990 (ibid.). The drop-off was most dramatic in the years 1970–76.

Nikkeijin who had previously worked as a broker estimated that only 20 percent of workplace injuries were officially reported.

Another indication of underreporting may lie in the rate of compliance of workplaces to labor standards. In 1992, of 154,109 workplaces inspected by the Labor Standards Bureau throughout the country, 90,250, or 58.6 percent, were found to be in violation of labor standards. In the auto industry, which was the primary sector for Nikkeijin in Japan, the rate of violation was even higher—64.9 percent (Rōdōshō rōdō kijunkyoku 1992, 26–27).[8]

Among Japanese, the discourse on community and responsibility at work sometimes represented the company as a "community of destiny" *(unmei no kyōdōtai)*. According to such a vision, Japanese workers dedicated and in some cases sacrificed themselves to their firms, especially when the firm's viability depended on it. Although larger firms could more readily guarantee employment in ways that smaller firms could not, it was at the less stable, smaller firms that I sometimes found a remarkable commitment to the firm among workers. In one factory that had hired a number of Nikkeijin workers, the Japanese staff had suffered various injuries over the years. A section chief had lost the tip of her index finger. This section chief's husband was missing most of one arm. The division chief had lost one of his fingers, and the company president himself had lost four fingers on his left hand. These accidents had occurred over many years, including times when safety procedures had been looser. More recently, however, one worker had injured two fingers, and another had lost his entire hand. These workers had not brought charges against the firm, for if they had, the firm would have been bankrupted several times over by now.[9]

Individual sacrifice for the larger community of the firm may have resonated with national ideologies of sacrifice. Emphasizing the sacrifice that Japanese soldiers have made for the nation since the Meiji period, Naoki Sakai writes that "the history of modern Japan is nothing but a history in which a national community was formed as the community of 'unnatural' death" (1991, 187). In practical terms, this may have meant that some manufacturing workers knowingly accepted working without safety sensors if that could increase production. Those who had cast their lots with their

---

[8] A breakdown of the violations showed that in 1991, 26.7 percent involved working hours (e.g. surpassing legal daily or weekly limits), 12.1 percent involved wages, 20.3 percent concerned employment conditions (e.g. use of employment brokers in sectors for which they were not permitted), 27.2 percent involved safety standards, and 13.7 percent concerned health standards (Rōdōshō rōdō kijunkyoku 1992, 26–27).

[9] See Christena Turner (1991, 1995) for an account of the difficult yet occasionally successful process by which workers at small firms could develop a worker-centered consciousness as opposed one centered on their obligations to their firm.

firm, who were willing to risk their own health to ensure the viability of the firm, were not likely to think of pursuing punitive damage claims when they were injured. Discourses emphasizing goodwill between employers and employees and a sense of community in the workplace encouraged amicable reconciliation between accident victims and their managers. Managers made efforts to keep injured workers on staff, even if they were no longer as productive as they had been.

Unlike her Japanese coworkers, Anna Fujita, a Nikkeijin worker who had lost three fingers at the factory where so many of her Japanese colleagues and managers had been injured, did not reconcile with her managers. Although she eventually received a sizable indemnity from accident insurance, when I interviewed her three years after the accident, she was still very bitter about the experience and hoped I could help her sue her managers. Was this because she did not share Japanese attitudes toward the primacy of "community"? As in the case of Vanessa, Anna's bitterness and anger stemmed from the cold treatment she received after the accident. The managers' initial unwillingness to help her file the paperwork necessary for her to receive an indemnity had made it impossible for her to reconcile with her managers. Moreover, their defensiveness after the accident did not allow them to express remorse in a form recognizable to Anna.

Gilberto Honda

When I met Gilberto, I noticed as he extended his right hand to shake mine that the top joint of his thumb was missing. We became good friends shortly after I arrived in Hamamatsu, but I never asked him about his thumb until it came up in a conversation about his experience as a member of Mahikari, one of Japan's many new religions. Members of Mahikari would approach people in public places and ask them if they would like to be purified. Reciting the name of the religion's founder, they would raise a hand and direct a purifying energy stream from its palm toward the foreheads of whoever had accepted the offer of purification (see Davis 1980). In our discussion, Gilberto said he had not realized at the time how dangerous this procedure was. When he performed it, the energy stream connecting him to those he was purifying apparently had created a channel through which evil spirits inhabiting those others entered his body. Gilberto explained that eventually he was possessed simultaneously by as many as fifty evil spirits, and that this led to a series of misfortunes culminating in the accident in which he lost part of his thumb. By the time I got to know him, two years had passed since Gilberto had quit Mahikari. He said that he had cleansed himself spiritually and that he was in robust health. He said the world in general was undergoing a spiritual cleansing.[10]

In the context of a formal interview, one year after he told me about the evil spirits that had inhabited him, Gilberto gave me a very different account of the accident in which he lost a part of his thumb. He described in detail the events leading up to the accident and placed the burden of responsibility on his managers rather than on evil spirits. The accident had occurred when he was tired and anxious in part because his supervisor had been harassing him, trying to get him to work faster than he was capable at the time. Gilberto said that he was working frantically but that his section chief still pushed him to work faster. Gilberto described this section chief as "very neurotic, extremely rude, and very strict" *(muito neurótico, super stúpido, e muito exigente)*, and noted that the Japanese workers were not fond of him either. Most important, Gilberto noted that he would not have lost his thumb had the machines at which he worked been equipped with legally mandatory safety sensors. The machines at Gilberto's workstation were equipped with sensors, but he said they were not functional; even if they had been, he said, they would not have been turned on. Several weeks earlier, he had asked about the sensors, but his boss did not give him a straight answer; consequently, Gilberto resigned himself to working without them.

On the morning of the accident, Gilberto's section chief kept him at his workstation during his five-minute break period, demonstrating how the job was supposed to be done and barking at him to work faster. Gilberto became flustered and upset, but nevertheless attempted to increase his speed. Only a few minutes later, as he was struggling to fit a tire into one machine, an air gun hanging overhead bounced against a switch and the machine clamped down on his thumb. He said he started losing consciousness and staggered backward toward another machine with blades that would have sliced him into thin strips if the Peruvian working at the next station had not rushed over and pulled him away.

He acknowledged that an ambulance arrived at the factory quickly. His section chief seemed to feel very guilty, apologizing profusely and accompanying him in the ambulance to the hospital. The section chief told Gilberto that such an accident had never occurred before in the factory. An agent from the broker through which Gilberto was employed soon joined them at the hospital to see how he was. While he was at home convalescing, various

---

[10] Higuchi Naoto suggests that Mahikari has attracted new members among Nikkeijin suffering mental and physical ills working in Japan (Higuchi 1998, 166, 173 [footnote 12]). The case of Gilberto indicates that continued participation of these new members may in part depend on the efficacy of Mahikari rituals. If their problems continue or intensify after joining, new members may be inclined to try another religion or practice.

people from his firm and employment agency visited him with presents, mostly food. It seemed that reconciliation may have been possible.

Gilberto initially may have been inclined to reconcile, but before long he became convinced that his managers' apologies were not sincere. When he returned to work three weeks after the accident, all the old and dysfunctional sensors had been replaced by new ones. Gilberto said that when inspectors from the Labor Standards Inspection Office visited the firm, his managers attributed the accident to his own distraction. The inspectors were apparently satisfied with the managers' explanation and did not bother interviewing Gilberto.

Labor Standards Law required manufacturers to equip their presses and other machinery with safety sensors that would immediately stop the machines' moving parts when someone got too close. Some managers turned off these sensors or pressured workers not to use them in order to achieve higher production. One Nikkeijin explained that if the sensors that were attached to his press were turned on, he would have had to stand two steps away, but when they were turned off, he could work right up against the machine. As soon as the stamping block started to rise, he could reach for the part and replace it with a fresh piece of metal. With sensors turned on, he could make at maximum 1,500 parts in a day. With them off, he could make twice that amount. Some Nikkeijin accepted whatever their managers asked of them because of their own unfamiliarity with Japanese labor standards and with the risk involved in the work. Others did so because they didn't want to jeopardize their jobs. Combined with the long hours of overtime work that Nikkeijin sought and competitive pressure from other workers, pressure from management contributed to the sidelining of workplace safety.[11]

The visit by labor standards inspectors may have been cursory because of their enormous workload. In 1995, there were 33,281 businesses (*jigyōsho*) in Hamamatsu, employing a total of 369,836 people. The Hamamatsu LSIO had only thirty-one people on staff at the time. Despite its unrelenting workload, its staff had been reduced by several members in the past few years. In 1991, Hamamatsu inspectors visited 851 businesses and found violations in 66.6 percent. In 1992, they visited 878 and found violations in 52.1 percent. In 1993, they visited 852 and found violations in 49.1 percent. In 1994, they visited 1,043 and found violations in 55.5 percent.[12] Industries that tended to have more accidents were visited more regularly, as were

---

[11] Demand for overtime work is a characteristic of migrants who set earnings goals and plan to return home after reaching the goals (Piore 1979, 95–98).

[12] These statistics were provided by officials at the LSIO in Hamamatsu during an interview in July 1997.

specific businesses that had a record of accidents. Nevertheless, under-staffing made it difficult for inspectors to reach more than a small fraction of all workplaces each year. It also meant that the office could not actively disseminate knowledge about its services to the general public, let alone to foreigners.

To Gilberto, his managers' dissimulation indicated that their expressions of remorse may in fact have been efforts to placate him and to minimize the possibility of financial damage to the firm. With the help of a group of Japanese advocates for foreign workers, he was eventually able to enroll retroactively in the legally mandatory accident insurance his broker had failed to provide. Four months later, he received an indemnity of roughly 100,000 yen (roughly $10,000) and then quit the firm.

Before the formal interview, I had interpreted Gilberto's account of spirit possession as a mystification of the responsibility of his managers to ensure a safe workplace. His account thus both intrigued me and disturbed me. I suspected that by transferring the responsibility for the accident from the managers to the spirits, Gilberto had forgone a legal settlement that may have provided him with greater financial compensation and forced more significant improvements in workplace safety at his factory.[13]

During my formal interview with him, however, Gilberto placed responsibility for the accident squarely on the shoulders of the firm. In two contexts, Gilberto had offered me strikingly different explanations for his misfortune. At the time of his accident, mental and physical exhaustion and uncertainty about the legal system in Japan had dissuaded Gilberto from seeking punitive damages. Gilberto's account of spirit possession may not have been an indication of his mystification so much as an expression of his general feeling of alienation in Japanese society. He experienced some Japanese workplaces as oppressive, grueling, and overly regimented in comparison with the clerical position at the Brazilian bank where he had worked for many years before going to Japan. It was through his account of spirit possession that Gilberto was able to make a broader critique of the exclusionary aspects of Japanese society and its impact on Nikkeijin migrants such as himself (see Taussig 1980). By quitting Mahikari and purging spirits

---

[13] There was precedent for foreign workers winning such suits. Tezuka Kazuaki describes one successful case in his book on foreigners and the law in Japan. In September 1992, a Tokyo court found a company negligent in the case of a Pakistani who lost the upper joint of his right index finger in a bookbinding machine that was not equipped with the required safety features. He received about 1,900,000 yen (equivalent to roughly $19,000 at the time) through the standard workplace accident insurance. He then brought suit against the company for violation of Labor Standards Law and received more than 2,500,000 yen compensation calculated according to a combination of the wages he was making at the time of the accident in Japan and the wages he had made at his factory job in Pakistan before coming to Japan. Another roughly 2,500,000 yen was awarded as "consolation money" (*isharyō*) (Tezuka 1995, 233–37).

that had inhabited him, Gilberto may also have helped himself recover from the psychological trauma of the accident.

Claudia and Marcos Kussakawa

The cases of Gilberto and Vanessa involved Nikkeijin who were unwilling to reconcile with their managers because of the way they were treated after their accidents. In Nikkeijin eyes, managers' failure to express remorse after an accident, their refusal to admit responsibility, or their unwillingness to help the injured worker receive an indemnity from accident insurance constituted a provocation that had to be acted upon (see Linger 1992). When Nikkeijin were treated with greater respect, however, they were able to reconcile.

Claudia and Marcos Kussakawa were a Nikkeijin couple in their mid-forties with children in kindergarten and second grade. They worked in separate factories but each had lost a part of a middle finger at work just two days apart. Two years later, both of them continued to work at the factories where they had suffered their accidents. Several factors help explain why they reconciled with their managers and stayed on at work while others did not.

Claudia explained that her firm provided all the assistance she needed when the accident occurred. Her managers took her to the hospital, paid the bill, and promptly took care of the paperwork that allowed her to receive an indemnity from workplace accident insurance. She was able to stay in the hospital for a full week, during which time people from the firm collected a sympathy payment *(mimaikin)* for her. Each of Claudia's thirty coworkers chipped in 1,000 yen ($10), and the firm's management contributed 100,000 yen, bringing the total to 130,000 ($1,300), an amount that made this informal gesture of sympathy significant. The firm also paid her wages for the three months she stayed at home after the accident.

The press at which Claudia was injured had not been equipped with sensors at the time of the accident. When she eventually returned to work, sensors had been installed, but Claudia did not interpret this improvement as an attempt on the part of management to cover up their liability for the accident. She noted that the owner of the firm and his wife had both lost fingers more than ten years previously working on machines that were far older than those currently being used.

Aside from the owners, Claudia knew no one else who had suffered an accident at her factory. The sympathy money, salary for the months she spent recuperating, and prompt processing of the indemnity payment probably all contributed to Claudia's willingness to reconcile with the firm. Claudia interpreted her managers' and coworkers' actions as expressions of their good intent. In her eyes, they did all they could for her, and they made room for her when she asked to be rehired.

Unlike many other Nikkeijin, including her husband, who worked through employment brokers, Claudia was a direct employee of the firm where she worked. Although Claudia had been working at the firm for only four months when she was injured, her managers and coworkers considered her a member of the workplace community enough to extend to her sincere gestures of care.

Brokered workers, too, were occasionally treated well enough that they could reconcile with the firm in which they had suffered accidents. Claudia's husband, Marcos, provides one such example. He told me, however, that he was fortunate to have gotten his broker's cooperation. Claudia noted that even though Marcos's broker was unusually good, not all workers got the same treatment:

> Those who work for brokers, not in my case, but in his [pointing to Marcos], the factory doesn't take any responsibility, doesn't even want to know, wants the broker to act and take care of it. In his case, the broker acted, and he got what he got. Very soon afterwards, another worker injured his finger as well, and the broker didn't even want to know about it. They said that they had already done it for Marcos and couldn't do another. . . . So the other worker, he couldn't do anything because having two workers getting hurt in the same factory in a short period of time would cause problems for the broker. So this guy didn't receive anything. . . . He didn't lose or cut his finger. It just became twisted.

Claudia commented that most brokers:

> say that they will give you assistance, take you to the hospital, but no one receives any indemnity. They stall and stall, give one excuse or another—they are all mafia—they pay nothing. And so you have people without fingers and without any compensation. There are so many cases of this. So many cases! So many cases of people who lost a finger and didn't receive! We were lucky to receive.

The awareness that other Nikkeijin may have had much greater difficulties than he did may have helped Marcos accept his own situation. In Claudia's case, she was able to reconcile with her managers at least in part because she felt like a member of the workplace community and interpreted their actions after the accident as indicative of responsible and caring behavior.

The interactions between Claudia and her employer fits a pattern that some social scientists have found more widely within Japanese society. Wagatsuma and Rosett argue that Japanese culture encourages apology in favor of either legal action or physical violence as a means of reestablishing

[85]

social harmony (Wagatsuma and Rosett 1986). John Haley concurs, writing that both the Japanese legal system and underlying cultural values are directed more toward reconciliation, while the U.S. legal system is directed more toward determination of guilt through adversarial conflict. Not only do expressions of remorse generally reduce fines and other penalties in Japanese courts, but also a high number of criminal code violations are never prosecuted because suspects express remorse and victims grant forgiveness (Haley 1986, 501). In the United States people avoid apologizing for fear that an apology would be used as evidence of liability; in Japan, however, apologies consistently have the effect of reducing or eliminating liability. The interactions between Claudia and Marcos and their employers showed that foreigners, in this case Nikkeijin, could reconcile with their employers in much the way that many Japanese workers have. Likewise, certain circumstances may motivate injured Japanese workers to confront their firms.

Shimura Satomi's Son, Shūzo

Shimura Satomi was a Japanese divorcée in her mid-forties when I interviewed her at a community center near her home in Iwata, the town just east of Hamamatsu. About eight months had passed since her son, Shūzo, lost half of his middle and ring fingers and the tip of his index finger, all on his right hand. Satomi had been somewhat worried about letting her son work in a factory. Whenever Shūzo came home from work, Satomi would ask him what he had been assigned to do that day. Initially, he was given a variety of jobs that were not dangerous. Eventually, however, he was switched to the presses. Shūzo reassured her, saying, "It's all right . . . don't worry . . . the press, when something happens, the machines stop moving, so it's all right. Mother, don't worry." After a few weeks, Shūzo was shifted to work with another person on a press that was having difficulty. This press was computer operated. It would regularly get stuck at one point in the process, and someone would have to remove the pressed sheet metal by hand and then reactivate the computer. Shūzo's job was to remove the piece by hand.

The accident occurred on Shūzo's first day on this press. The other operator reactivated the computer while Shūzo's hand was still in the press. Satomi emphasized that "this was clearly the responsibility of the firm." A coworker from the firm took her son to the hospital, where he stayed for a week to recuperate. Although the firm's owner and several others from the firm attended while her son was in surgery, no one visited him at the hospital afterward. On the day he was released from the hospital, the coworker who had taken him there visited him at home and brought a little sympathy money *(omimai no okane)*, but it was just a little—probably out of his own pocket. It was not an official gesture by the firm. It was nothing the like collection of money Claudia received from all of her coworkers and managers.

Satomi eventually called the owner of the firm where her son had been injured and mentioned that she was thinking about talking to people at the Labor Standards Inspection Office. He became flustered and promised to make various provisions (*ironna hoshō o shimasu kara*), trying to convince her that such measures were unnecessary. More time passed without any follow-up, however, so she decided to go to the LSIO. It turned out that the firm had filed the mandatory accident report without which her son would not receive any money from accident insurance. Satomi noted, however, that the most important detail was missing in the report—"that the machine wasn't functioning properly and that he had to manipulate things manually, and that the other worker on the machine was a bit slow in the head" (*atama ga sukoshi hikui hito*).

Four months after the accident, Shūzo had not returned to work, and yet he had not officially quit or been fired. Satomi wanted to negotiate compensation before having her son formally leave the firm. The firm, however, avoided her requests for clarification on compensation, and just requested that her son resign and turn in the government-sponsored employee insurance document he had been issued when he first started working there. Satomi refused to comply. In May, she learned from the local office of the national Social Insurance Agency (Shakai Hoken Chō) that the firm had removed Shūzo from its roster, implying that he was no longer officially affiliated with the firm.

Satomi was outraged by these actions on the part of the firm. She speculated about the owner's motives:

> My son had worked for only twenty days [before the accident], so probably the owner wanted to take care of the worker who had been with the firm a long time. . . . This made me mad. My son had gotten injured. He could go out, but he was still bandaged. I took him with me and went to the firm. I said to the owner that he had never come to pay condolences (*nannimo mimai ni konai*), that he had never apologized (*ayamari mo shinai*) to my son—that since he had taken the side of the other worker, he hadn't made any apology. This is what I told him.

In her narrative of her interactions with managers after the accident, Satomi initially was interested only in an indemnity from accident insurance. She was not interested in getting money from the firm itself. Satomi described a process of interaction centering on the managers' unwillingness to express remorse and their rebuff of each of her inquiries, through which her relationship with them underwent a fundamental change. The firm's avoidance of forthright discussion about the accident, its unwillingness to help her son file the forms necessary to receive an indemnity, its actions to remove him from their rosters, and its lack of sincere expression of remorse, sympathy, or apology all spurred Satomi to demand retributive justice through the legal system. Once motivated to do so, Satomi pinpointed the responsibility of the firm and demanded full compensation. With the help of the volunteer group, Hamamatsu Overseas Laborers Solidarity, her son finally received 2.8 million yen (roughly $28,000) from accident insurance one year after the accident; two months later, he received a much more satisfying 2.5 million yen ($25,000) in punitive damages (*shazaikin*, literally "apology crime money") from the firm itself.

The cases of Shūzo and Claudia counter the stereotypes that Japanese prefer reconciliation while foreigners prefer adversarial confrontation. The specific circumstances surrounding an accident often revealed why the injured party was or was not able to reconcile with managers. Although the outcomes of Claudia's and Shūzo's cases were very different, both workers shared the same moral compass: retributive justice was sought only after the desire for a just reconciliation was frustrated. Both Nikkeijin and Japanese could respond positively to sincere expressions of remorse and care, expressions that acknowledged their dignity as workers and as human beings.

Sincere Apologies and Just Communities

The function of apology in bringing about reconciliation between aggrieved parties is sometimes thought to be peculiar to Japanese society. Wagatsuma and Rosett write that apologies may even be preferable to offers of financial compensation there: "[I]f an offender is too willing to offer reparation without indicating his repentance and expressing apology, the response of other Japanese is likely to be unaccepting" (Wagatsuma and Rosett 1986, 473). Furthermore, in an article on automobile accident compensation in Japan, Takao Tanase writes that the resolution of conflict and the restoration of amicable ties depend not just on the act of apology, but also on its sincerity. He writes:

> If an injurer takes an "insincere" attitude by failing to inquire after the injured party at the hospital or fails to offer condolences to the deceased's relatives, the injured party or his relatives will harden their attitude, and negotiations will become very difficult or may even deadlock. (Tanase 1990, 678)

Tanase adds that when apologies are not readily forthcoming, the "injured party himself . . . keeps demanding the injurer to express his 'sincere' apologies for the accident" (ibid., 679). Often it is impossible to know whether someone is sincerely remorseful, but if the apology itself is expressed with language that emphasizes sincerity, it constitutes a meaningful effort at restoring social harmony, a primary value in the Japanese context, according to Tanase, Wagatsuma and Rosett.

When significant damages are at issue, however, Tanase notes, the only way to demonstrate sincerity may be through generous compensation (ibid., 678). This is what Frank Upham found in his account of the infamous Minamata mercury poisoning case. Since the 1950s, thousands of people living near the city of Minamata in southern Japan have suffered neurological damage and many have died after eating fish contaminated by the toxic runoff from Chisso Corporation's chemical plant. Chisso initially tried to settle the case out of court by making a sympathy payment worth a small fraction of formal compensation *(hoshōkin)*, an offer that was rejected by the victims and their relatives (Upham 1987, 30–37).

The accident cases presented in this chapter each involved serious injury, and three of the injured had actively pursued legal channels for compensation or had otherwise fallen out with their employers. None of them indicated that money was the issue, however; their dignity had been compromised by their managers' lack of remorse. For Gilberto, this lack of remorse became apparent when his managers lied to labor inspectors and assigned blame for the accident to him. Vanessa would not have brought charges had not her manager provoked her through his insensitive and rude treatment. Satomi's outrage came from the firm's unwillingness to communicate with her let alone express its condolences following Shūzo's accident. The stories of these injured workers indicate that sincere expressions of remorse in the form of respectful treatment and cooperation in arranging indemnities from accident insurance might have gone a long way toward satisfying the workers. Only when these efforts were not forthcoming did some of the injured decide to pursue legal channels to punish what they interpreted as intolerable attitudes on the part of their managers.

Some Japanese felt that migrants were self-interested and had an impoverished sense of community that contradicted the privileged place that group solidarity has had in Japanese society. One employment broker also accused Brazilians of exaggerating injuries, even when they were not work-related, in order to get paid days off and other benefits. Anna Fujita, the Brazilian who had lost three fingers at the firm where the majority of the Japanese workers seemed to have lost some body part, indicated that these constructions of Brazilian self-interest were terribly inaccurate when it came to the more serious accidents. She had received an indemnity from accident insurance, but was so revolted by the idea that a fixed price could be calculated for her mutilation that she let the indemnity payments, which were directly deposited into her bank account every four months, accumulate for two years without touching them. Eventually she decided to send most of the money to her aging parents in Brazil.

To what extent, then, were Nikkeijin attitudes toward justice and community different from those of Japanese? The term *unmei no kyōdōtai* (community of destiny) indicates how some Japanese workers, as well as managers, have framed the link between their fates and those of their firms. At Anna's firm, the five Japanese who had been injured over a long period apparently felt that increased production was worth the risk involved in working without safety sensors. These workers sank or swam with their firm. Where mutilation has been normalized as a part of the job, we witness the pathological side of "benevolence" and "goodwill." Durkheim wrote of social pathology in terms of the alienation of individuals in modern industrial society, but in the example of this firm—where most workers and managers were injured over many years—we have people who have suffered for the sake of a community ideal. They suffered precisely because they were incorporated within the community of the workplace, not because they were alienated from it.

These cases indicate that Nikkeijin too, if accorded respect and sympathy after accidents, may have been willing to be a part of such communities. The narratives of injured workers reveal that Japanese and Nikkeijin interacted with managers after accidents according to similar moral principles. Those whose managers expressed sincere remorse were able to reconcile. The case of Claudia illustrates the fulfillment of Nikkeijin desire for such a community. Those who did not receive the treatment they expected, as in the cases of Vanessa, Gilberto, and Shūzo, were motivated to quit and to take legal action against their former employers.

The case of Satomi's son, Shūzo, indicates that, contrary to cultural stereotypes, when Japanese were subjected to treatment similar to that which many Nikkeijin suffered, they too could be driven to demand retributive justice in the courts. If greater numbers of Nikkeijin appear not to have been able to reconcile with their managers, the explanation may be that managers tended to apologize and to express remorse to their full time Japanese workers more than they did to their brokered Nikkeijin workers. As marginalized brokered workers, Nikkeijin were marked as outsiders to the workplace community, and thus were denied the treatment accorded insiders. Their status as brokered workers meant not only that Nikkeijin were excluded from the social community of the workplace and denied the apologies that were necessary for them to maintain their dignity, but that they frequently lacked health and accident insurance or stability in employment during economic downturns.

Nikkeijin marginalization in the Japanese workforce may have a silver lining. Although they were angered and hurt by their managers' lack of remorse, marginalized workers were more likely to take the managers to court and ultimately to lead to safer workplaces. The Japanese legal system was another institutional context that Nikkeijin were still learning how to navigate. Their efforts, and those of similarly marginalized Japanese, may eventually contribute to the evolution of just communities—communities that both maintain respectful interactions among their members and are protected by safety standards.

Some Nikkeijin were intent on making as much money in as short a time as possible and then returning home to their families and friends in Brazil. More, however, had social needs that went beyond the purely economic dimension during their residence in Japan. Although a few like Claudia, who was hired directly by her managers, were able to find community in the workplace, many more Nikkeijin were marginalized through a system of employment brokers that excluded them from membership within workplace communities. Where did these Nikkeijin experience community in Japan? Many built their own communities within Brazilian ethnic enclaves, formed by a network of churches, restaurants, stores, and informal gathering places for barbecues and other activities. In the next chapter, I explore one such locus of Nikkeijin community, a Brazilian culture center that flourished for two years in Hamamatsu.

[5]

Money and Community at the Brazilian Culture Center

Luís Horikawa, the founder of the short-lived Brazilian culture center in Hamamatsu, explained the inspiration behind his center with this story:

> In the dry northeastern part of Brazil, there was a village of faith whose residents were diligent workers. It had a church, a community center, and many places for children to play. One year, the rains did not come. Crops failed and dust swept through the village. Day after day the sun beat down on the people who gathered in the plaza to pray for rain. Some became desperate as they prayed and prayed, crying and walking to and fro. But in their midst there was one little girl holding an umbrella opened over herself as she prayed. Her faith was stronger than the others', and it was her faith that brought the rains and ended the drought.

The story of faith in a benevolent providence is one that has appeared in many guises throughout Brazil.[1] Luís interpreted the story to mean not just that one must have faith in providence, but that benevolent providence was in part dependent on one's faith in oneself. In telling me this story within the Japanese context, Luís proclaimed the importance of a Brazilian identity in Japan and of the role that his center had in promoting it.

Luís thought that too many Nikkeijin working in Japan were fixated on money and had lost a part of their humanity. In this respect, he shared the negative evaluation of Nikkeijin migrants held by many Japanese. In a more important respect, however, his understanding was different. He did not

---

[1] I thank Jeffrey Lesser for pointing this out. See Lesser (1999) for a discussion of the rhetorical claims to Brazilian identity made by early Japanese migrants to Brazil.

consider self-interest to be a Brazilian cultural trait but rather an effect of being a Brazilian migrant. He thought it was important for Nikkeijin to respect Japanese practices and to abide by certain rules, but he did not expect them to forgo their Brazilian heritage. He intended for his culture center to help Nikkeijin learn to have faith in themselves, to take pride in Brazilian culture, to respect Japanese culture, and to make friends. After all, he said, money comes and money goes. Friendship and cultural knowledge, on the other hand, were things one could hold on to. They enriched one's life in a way money alone could not.

Although certain local governments, including Hamamatsu's, have made significant efforts to improve services for foreigners, many Nikkeijin felt alienated from Japanese society. Many were initially willing to sacrifice socially rich lives in Brazil for short-term economic gain in Japan. Most Nikkeijin went to Japan with the intention of working between one and three years. They planned to return to Brazil with money to better take care of their families, build homes, buy cars, start businesses, or retire in comfort. Many did so, but many others extended their stays in Japan despite the deepening recession there. Not even the stabilization of the Brazilian economy was enough to bring about a decline in the number of Brazilian residents in Japan (see Tsuda 1999).

Nikkeijin were not settling because they felt at home in Japan. The fact that they were of Japanese ancestry did not lead to their smooth assimilation as immigration officials had expected. Although some Nikkeijin became accustomed to work and life in Japan, the longer they stayed, the more they began to conceive of themselves as a distinct Brazilian minority within Japan. Daniel Linger writes that for Brazilians in Japan, eating a Brazilian meal is an intrinsically Brazilian experience, while having the same meal in any restaurant in Brazil would be merely a culinary one (Linger 2001). Takeyuki Tsuda has described a carnival parade put on by Japanese Brazilians in the town of Ōizumi, Gumma Prefecture, most of whom had little if any interest in samba before coming to Japan (see Tsuda 2000). Luís's Brazilian culture center was just one of many expressions of an increasingly widespread feeling among Nikkeijin that they were not "Japonês."

In the context of the Brazilian culture center, and increasingly in newspaper articles, the more inclusive label "Brasileiro" was used in place of the more ethnically specific "Nikkeijin." In this chapter, I give preference when appropriate to the term "Brazilian" in place of "Nikkeijin" to reflect increased salience of the oppositional identification between Brazilian and Japanese. Of course, there were ongoing distinctions among Brazilians in Japan between Nikkeijin and non-Nikkeijin spouses or adoptees of Nikkeijin; between "pure" Nikkeijin and "mestizos"; between nisei and sansei; and

[93]

between those who spoke Japanese fluently and those who spoke very little. In the context of the workplace, these distinctions, especially the distinction based on language fluency, were significant and may have been the source of tensions among Brazilians. As illustrated by the case of Mirella (chapter 4), those who received special treatment in the workplace because of their language facility, especially those who were promoted to work as translators or supervisors, often suffered the censure of other Brazilians. After working in an employment broker's office for a year and a half and being forced to constantly mediate between Brazilian workers and Japanese managers, Mirella was eager to return to the factory floor.

In other contexts, such as the Brazilian culture center, distinctions among Brazilians were subsumed within the larger opposition between Brazilians and Japanese. Some distinctions remained, but if anything, those who were in some sense more closely identified with things Brazilian had higher status. Although Luís himself was a "pure" Nikkeijin *(Nikkeijin puro)*, the majority of teachers he recruited for various classes there were either mestizos or non-Nikkeijin. In light of Nikkeijin marginalization in the workplace and the stigma attached to their jobs, Luís's center helped them take pride in themselves and in their Brazilian heritage. Although the center has closed, it symbolized a growing urge among Nikkeijin and other Brazilians to express a unmistakably Brazilian identity in Japan.

Migrants, Money, and the Redefinition of Goals

In a public lecture at Hamamatsu International Communication and Exchange (HICE) in February 1994, a Japanese diplomat who had recently returned from a post in Brazil discussed differences between Japanese and Brazilian cultures and pointed to areas in which Japan could learn from Brazil. Throughout his lecture, he characterized Brazil and Japan as absolute opposites *(sei hantai no kuni)*. Although Japan had been guided by the three principles of efficiency, thoroughness *(nandemo kanzen ni suru)*, and homogeneity, Brazil could best be characterized by enjoyment and variety. He was proud of Japanese achievements but said that Japanese needed to learn how to relax, to have fun, and to cultivate a spiritually rich lifestyle. In these regards, he concluded, Japanese could look to Brazil.

In the late 1980s and early 1990s, however, many Brazilian migrants in Japan were not so carefree. Like many migrant workers throughout the world, they sought as much overtime as possible, planning to return home when they achieved the target earnings they had set for themselves (see Piore 1979, 95–98). Their goal orientation and dedication to work was much appreciated by Japanese employers. One Brazilian, João Okuno, described his first year in Japan as a time when he focused exclusively on making money to send back to Brazil. He made roughly 300,000 yen (about $3,000 at the time) per month, and spent only 20,000 on the bare essentials. He ate almost exclusively in the subsidized company cafeteria, making instant ramen for himself on weekends when the cafeteria was closed. Brazilian migrants' appetite for work pleased Japanese managers who, in order to meet high production demands at the time, needed a workforce hungry for overtime.

In 1994 and 1995, the weekly newspaper *Tudo Bem* published a series of essays by readers, most of whom espoused the same attitude toward work in Japan and eventual return to Brazil that João did. Some of the *Tudo Bem* essays were later collected and published in a volume titled *Dekassegui—Os Exilados Economicôs* [Dekasegi—The Economic Exiles]. The author of one essay was particularly patriotic:

> [T]he greatest dream of all of us Brazilians living abroad is to honor our agreements here in Japan, and to return as rapidly as possible and continue working with all our energy, faith and hope so that fatal collapse does not occur to the benevolent and marvelous giant known as Brazil. More than ever, it is the hour to be Brazilian. (Sai Media Kenkyūkai 1995, 97)

A number of other essays, however, expressed revulsion with what the authors considered the Brazilian system of injustice and the government's incompetence. One wrote that "criminality, insecurity, inflation, and uncertainty" made her decide to leave the country. Many described the difficulties they had encountered working in Japan; they cited abusive comments of their Japanese coworkers and a general feeling that Japanese lacked warmth. Although many also described their time in Japan as enriching—as an adventure full of challenges they had overcome—none of the authors portrayed their stays as more than a temporary exile. More than anything else, they emphasized the pain they suffered when they left their families behind and their desire to be reunited in Brazil.

Most people I knew expressed their desire to return eventually to Brazil. But during my fieldwork, I noticed that Brazilians increasingly conceived of staying in Japan beyond the one to three years they had initially planned. Some thought they may stay as long as five or more years, and a few hinted at the possibility of staying permanently in Japan (see Yamanaka 2000). To be able to imagine such extended periods in Japan indicated a greater possibility of eventual settlement. Most Brazilians I talked to still proclaimed their intention of going back to Brazil, but increasingly they began to conceive of more complex relationships with both Japan and Brazil.

The Portuguese language media offered a window through which to view this shift in discourse. In his comprehensive survey of Portuguese language media in Japan, Japanese Brazilian anthropologist Angelo Ishi interviewed the founders of each of the first three Portuguese language newspapers established.[2] *The International Press* and *Folha Mundial* had been established in late 1991, followed by *Tudo Bem* in early 1992. Each of the founders stated that one of the main reasons for starting his paper was the "hunger Brazilians felt for news of Brazil" (Ishi 1996, 105, 113, 118). Reading about Brazil and just seeing Portuguese in print helped Brazilians survive psychologically until they had made enough money and could leave Japan.

In addition to providing news from Brazil, however, each of these newspapers became important channels of other information for migrants, and eventually took leading roles in fostering a sense of community within the Japanese context (ibid., 133–41). In late 1995, a fourth Portuguese language newspaper, *Nova Visão*, began publication, proclaiming in an editorial on October 8, 1995, to be uniquely dedicated to the Brazilian community in Japan. The other papers provided news of Brazil as well as of the migrant community in Japan but *Nova Visão* was the first to give this Japanese news precedence over Brazilian news. The rhetoric of the new paper, in addition to the community-promoting functions that the other papers had already started to serve, indicated the extent to which Brazilian institutions and people had started to sink roots in Japan.

Nova Visão editorials revealed the paper's orientation toward longer-term Brazilian residents in Japan. In the seventh issue (November 19, 1995), the editorial criticized Brazilians who violated Japanese laws or conventions by littering, driving recklessly, and using illegal telephone cards. The editorial implied that such Brazilians were mostly recent migrants who lacked the respectful attitude of the "veterans"—those who had been in Japan several years and made efforts to accommodate Japanese standards of public behavior. The following week's editorial (November 26, 1995) announced that starting with that issue, the newspaper would publish at least one page of articles in Japanese, using a limited number of Chinese characters, for the benefit of Brazilians who were studying Japanese, as well as for Japanese who were interested in the Brazilian community.[3]

In its fourth issue (October 29, 1995), the *Nova Visão* editorial described in positive terms how "veteran" Brazilians in Japan were spending more on

---

[2] Ishi eventually became the chief editor of *Tudo Bem*, one of the Portuguese language newspapers published in Japan.

[3] *Tudo Bem* had previously included a Japanese language page but stopped doing so in February 1995 to rededicate itself as the paper "for Brazilians and by Brazilians" (Ishi 1996: 146). *The International Press* published only five editions of a Japanese language paper in 1992 before it stopped for lack of readership (ibid.:108).

consumer products and leisure activities. Although Brazilians in Japan continued to remit about $2 billion annually to Brazil through the latter 1990s (Vizentini 1998), those who decided to stay longer tended to give up overtime and night shift work in favor of more normal working hours and safer work conditions. Many began to reevaluate their goals and priorities as they discovered certain pleasures of life in Japan. It was not uncommon to hear of people who had taken trips to Okinawa or Hokkaido, or overseas to Bali or the United States. Their cramped apartments were crammed with stereos, TVS, VCRs, and sometimes even computers connected to the Internet, on which they created personal web pages with photos of themselves and friends, or entered "chat" rooms catering to Nikkeijin in both Japan and Brazil. Young Brazilians frequented amusement parks, bowling alleys, discos, and restaurants. Many held on to only a fraction of their earnings.

Some Japanese have asked what the goals of such Brazilians were. Why were they in Japan if not to save for their futures in Brazil? I interviewed a Japanese manager at a car-parts firm in summer 1997 who criticized Brazilians who discarded their initial goals and started spending their money on cars, drinking, and other diversions. Such Brazilians were likely to become a social problem, he said. His statements surprised me; when I had interviewed him two years previously, he had expressed his own desire for a life that went beyond a single-minded devotion to work. Capitalism thrives on competition, he had told me, with the strong doing well and the weak being left behind. In a reflective moment, however, he shook his head and sighed, "Money, money, money . . . it gets so distasteful" (*Kane, kane, kane . . . iya ni natchau*).

For him, the social ideals embodied within the concept of the Japanese employment system and long-term relations among groups of companies were just ideals, far removed from his own reality, and he seemed to be searching for fulfillment in a different arena. Nevertheless, he could not accept such a search for fulfillment among Brazilian residents in Japan.

Among Brazilians too, there was concern about juvenile delinquency, violent gangs, disappearances, and other social ills associated with migrant society. But there was no going back to the early days of intense overtime work and focus on savings. For one thing, the extreme austerity some migrants imposed on themselves early on could be maintained for only a limited time. João Okuno, who had claimed to have spent only 20,000 per month the first year he lived in Japan, explained that by the end of the year he had lost twenty kilograms, over 40 pounds. When I interviewed him, he had regained most if not all of his former weight, and espoused living more fully as a part of Japanese society. *Nova Visão's* October 29, 1995, editorial made a similar point in a discussion about consumerism among Brazilians in Japan:

It is not true that Brazilians today only think of saving money. It may have been so at the beginning of the immigration 'boom', but at the moment, although still a minority, many wish to live more comfortably in Japan.

Gradually, more and more Brazilians who had been in Japan four, five, or more years were becoming critical of short-term migrants' exclusive focus on earning money. João, reflecting on his own experience, characterized his initial focus on money as pathological. Love of one's work was not intrinsically problematic, he said, but there was something wrong with a work ethic that overwhelmed all the other pleasures of life.

Although Brazilians generally did not criticize other migrants as bitingly as Vanessa (chapter 4) had criticized her Japanese boss and his obsession with money, many did complain about such an obsession. In the late 1980s and early 1990s, Brazilians meeting for the first time had been preoccupied in knowing how much each other made per hour and how much overtime each other worked every day (see also Ishi 1994, 49). Gradually, however, more and more Brazilians began to criticize the fixation on making money.

Edivaldo Kishimoto explained that this was one reason he had few Brazilian friends in Japan. He complained that most Brazilians talked only about work, money, and girls. Gilberto Honda said much the same thing, although in reference specifically to the Brazilians he had met during the year and a half he worked in Toyama, where he had gone after his accident in a Hamamatsu factory. He was unhappy in Toyama because the Brazilians he met there talked only about money and Filipino girlfriends. Gilberto returned to Hamamatsu because the greater number of Brazilians made it easier for him to find like-minded friends there.

In establishing his culture center, Luís tapped into this critique of money obsession. He wanted his center to promote activities and relationships that transcended the cash nexus. Although he never filled out the paperwork necessary to register the center as a nonprofit organization (*centro cultural sem fins lucrativos*), that is how he wished to present it. He claimed it to be a haven from the contractual relationships that permeated most migrants' lives in Japan; by appealing to values more permanent and meaningful than those represented by money, he attempted to establish the center as a moral community. For that reason, the center may have been more comparable to the various Brazilian religious congregations established in Hamamatsu than to Brazilian restaurants and clubs.

"It is not a school," Luís would insist in reply to questions people had about the course offerings. His insistence on using the term "center" in place of "school" expressed his concern about accusations that he was peddling culture for profit. In his mind, culture and money belonged to two separate spheres of exchange. He spoke of how the center provided the space and structure around which a moral and artistic community could develop that was inclusive of people of all nationalities.

In practice, however, the center was always dominated by Brazilians. In addition, the center was not a pure realm of community apart from economy. It took a substantial amount of money to maintain—to pay the instructors, the utility bills, the rent, and Luís's living expenses. The students at the center paid for the courses they took, much as they would in a school. What haven from market forces Luís provided existed only for the instructors, and even that could not last indefinitely. Precisely in overemphasizing the center as a community free of the pollution of money, he created what he later called an unhealthy *"cultura de paternalismo"* (culture of paternalism) between himself and the instructors. The instructors became accustomed to having Luís maintain the center financially and were unwilling to cooperate when he eventually tried to redistribute some of the financial burden, leading eventually to the center's closing.

The fragility of the center evoked the ephemeral character of many Brazilian enterprises in Japan and of migrant life in general.[4] Some may interpret the conflicts that led to the center's collapse as indicative of Brazilians' inability to sustain community—evidence of their incompatibility with Japanese society. Such an interpretation would be misguided, however. The center's collapse resulted from a variety of factors unrelated to attitudes toward community.

The center's achievements revealed how Brazilians had started to define a place for themselves within Japan. The center exemplified the emergence among Brazilians of a long-term orientation toward life in Japan that defied the model of assimilation. The center served as an alternative community to the Japanese workplace communities from which Brazilians had generally been excluded. Its primary achievement was to provide an outlet for an increasingly widespread feeling among Brazilian Nikkeijin that they were not "Japonês." Although many Japanese stigmatized Brazilians, Luis's center helped its members to take pride in their Brazilian heritage.

The Space

Luís had made many Japanese acquaintances during his six years in Japan. Using his shy manners to his advantage, Luís had won the confidence

---

[4] Higuchi and Takahashi's survey of seventy-seven Brazilian businesses in Japan indicated that their number and diversity grew significantly between 1992 and 1997 (1998b). The study was based on a survey of existing business, however, and did not include any record of businesses that failed before the survey was conducted. The increase in number and diversity may not have been quite as dramatic during this period if failed businesses also had been taken into account.

of one Japanese, who agreed to be his guarantor.[5] This allowed him to rent an apartment, while most Brazilians had to live in company dormitories or apartments arranged for them by brokers. Another one of Luís's Japanese acquaintances, Sato Hideaki, eventually agreed to rent Luís a space for the culture center. The goal was to promote greater interaction and cultural understanding among Japanese, Brazilians, and other foreigners. Soon after he committed himself to the building, Luís called to give me a tour of the premises and to talk about his plans.

The building was in Hamamatsu's old downtown district. The large avenues that formed a grid in the reconstructed downtown soon gave way to small two-lane streets that zigzagged in different directions. Luís's new building was in a neighborhood just beyond the grid. The streets were narrow, and many were no more than two blocks long. In such neighborhoods, one easily loses one's sense of direction after turning from one street to another several times. The first time I tried to find the building, I got within a block or two but finally lost my way and had to call Luís from a pay phone and have him meet me.

The heavyset three-story building had thick ribs of concrete at two-meter intervals; the fortress-like appearance contrasted sharply with the majority of homes, built of wood and corrugated metal, that lined the street. From the second-floor ledge Luís had extended a plastic pole from which he hung the Brazilian flag. The pole was made of soft plastic; after a few days it curved limply, but still served as a landmark for first-time visitors. Considering the building's imposing exterior, I was surprised that it had an entranceway designed for people to take off their shoes, and that much of the building had wooden hallways connecting rooms with tatami mats, the finely woven reed mats used as flooring in some Japanese houses.[6] It was apparent that the interior had been designed as a high-class Japanese-style restaurant. The first floor had been a residence, possibly for the owner of the restaurant. Another entrance had led restaurant customers up a staircase to a sushi bar on the second floor. Across from the sushi bar was a raised space with tatami matting where people must have had meals seated around low tables.

---

[5]The immigration bureau did not issue long-term visas to foreigners without guarantors (*hoshōnin*) who agree to cover any expenses incurred by their wards during their stays in Japan. Landlords also did not rent apartments to either Japanese or foreigners without guarantors. Most commonly, employers acted as guarantors for foreigners, which almost always meant that a change of job involved a change of residence. A Brazilian who aspired to residential independence often could not do so for lack of alternate guarantors. Having one's own residence meant greater privacy and freedom from the inspections that brokers made from time to time, and not having to deal with a series of unknown roommates moving in and out. It meant greater overall autonomy from brokers.

[6]Rooms are often measured in terms of the numbers of mats they hold, six and eight being common sizes. Each mat is a little less than one meter in width and two in length.

The interior still maintained a certain elegance, although the tatami were frayed at the edges and discolored with age. The tiled floors on the second floor were chipped and cracked in places, and the kitchen and area behind the sushi counter were covered with an oily crud that had hardened over many years. Luís told me that the pipes were rusty, and when he turned on the faucet, the water ran a deep reddish brown for several seconds before gradually clearing. No one had lived in the building for nearly ten years. The external shell looked indestructible, but the interior clearly was not. Possibly because the building was several blocks beyond the main concentration of downtown restaurants, bars and clubs, the establishments that had occupied the building had not prospered.

Almost all of the windows faced east, and the concrete ribs cast shadows that prevented direct sunlight from entering past mid-morning. The years of neglect and lack of human habitation lent an eerie quality to the building. When he moved in, Luís invited a Brazilian commercial artist and his family to sublet the third floor. This family moved out before long, however, and Luís told me later that the artist claimed to have heard strange footsteps in the halls at night. He thought the house was haunted, and wondered whether a murder had taken place there long ago. Another visitor to the center commented that an especially narrow, long, and gloomy hallway on the first floor, lit only by one small incandescent light recessed into the ceiling, probably contained a portal into the netherworld through which spirits could travel. Luís was not concerned with this story, but several months after I had moved in, we began to hear footsteps scurrying over the first-floor ceiling. Using a flashlight to peer through a hatch at the top of a futon closet, we discovered a beautiful gray fox with a fluffy tail living in the crawl space between the first and second floors. Whether the building was inhabited by human spirits or fox spirits,[7] or whether just by humans and terrestrial foxes, I wondered whether Luís would be able to create the brighter atmosphere necessary to attract people to his culture center.

A Creative Community of Faith

Over the course of many conversations, I learned that Luís's inspiration for establishing the center had come from at least three sources. In addition to the story about a little girl's faith concerning rain, Luís mentioned being inspired by the model of Yuba, a commune established by Japanese in the

[7] In certain parts of Japan, families that had experienced dramatic increases in wealth were said to be possessed by fox spirits. Foxes were reputed to help family fortunes but also to corrupt and had the effect of stigmatizing the families they supposedly possessed.

interior of São Paulo state in Brazil,[8] and by the work of the Catholic congregation of Japanese in Hamamatsu. Each of these sources provided some sense of the kind of community that Luís wanted to build around his center. He wanted the center to offer a space for people to get together in an informal and relaxed way. Whereas a school implied a hierarchical relationship in which students paid for knowledge, a culture center offered the opportunity for the equal exchange of knowledge and the development of friendships among Japanese and Brazilians.

Japanese migrants to Brazil established many agricultural cooperatives that allowed them to buy materials in bulk at lower rates and to sell produce more efficiently. To some extent these cooperatives were based on a sense of ethnic solidarity, but rival factions, disparities in wealth, and movement in and out of the community were ever present (Staniford 1973, 24–27, 149–72).[9] Luís, however, emphasized the solidarity of the members of one commune whose members not only pooled all their resources and worked collectively on the land, but also cultivated the arts and had an active theater. It was this collaboration in the artistic and spiritual aspects of life that Luís wanted to re-create in his center.

Luís worked in an auto factory and lived in a company house with about ten other Brazilian workers his first three years in Japan. At that time, he had joined a Japanese Catholic congregation in Hamamatsu. He often declined his Japanese coworkers' invitations to socialize. He sought a wider community outside the workplace, one that he found at the Catholic church in Hamamatsu. Church volunteers taught Japanese to a variety of foreign workers, including Filipinos, Iranians, Peruvians, and Pakistanis, as well as Nikkeijin, and Luís made friends with many of them. Everyone spoke either English or Japanese. He told me that he had no close Brazilian friends at the time, but that the international community he had found at the church had been deeply satisfying.

The congregation had been located in the downtown neighborhood (Moto Uo-cho) where Luís later established the culture center, but eventually moved to an outlying district of Hamamatsu. The new building was more spacious and modern, but Luís felt it to be cold, and he lamented its inaccessibility for the majority of foreigners who didn't have cars. He commented that "the system of help [and the] . . . international community which the church created, the church itself destroyed" (*a sistema de ajuda, uma comunidade internacional que a igreja criou, a própria igreja de-*

---

[8] Karen Yamashita's novel *Brazil Maru* (1992) revolves around a fictionalized account of Yuba.

[9] Philip Staniford's monograph provides a detailed account of the role of the cooperative in social, economic, and political organization in the Japanese community of Tome Açu, in the northeastern state of Pará.

struiu). With this sense of regret and betrayal, he said his social world would probably have been much wider if he had accepted his Japanese coworkers' occasional invitations to play golf or go drinking. Having a strong network of Japanese friends was important, he said.

By the time I was living in Hamamatsu, Brazilians could hear Mass in Portuguese.[10] The Nikkeijin priest was active and popular within the migrant community. Luís commented that although this was good, it also took away one of the few positive contexts outside the workplace where Brazilians could engage with Japanese society. Brazilians and Japanese could interact at bars, discos, pachinko parlors, and restaurants, but such contexts were not conducive to the development of more than passing relationships.

I was sympathetic to Luís's desire to provide another kind of place for Brazilians, but I felt that he reiterated the distinction between his center and a school in a somewhat dogmatic and defensive fashion. His stance was in part related to the plans of the owner of the dominant Brazilian food and clothing store in town to offer classes in computers, Japanese and English languages, and guitar—all classes that Luís had already begun at his culture center. Luís stressed that the store's classes could teach technique, but they could not offer the vibrant and supportive cultural milieu that his center did. At its height of activity, his center indeed generated an enthusiasm difficult to reproduce in more formal classroom settings.

Weekends at the Center

Most of the center's activity was concentrated on the weekends. There were only sporadic classes or meetings on weekdays. Every other Tuesday evening, a small group of Brazilian students came to study kanji (Chinese characters used in Japanese writing) with a Japanese instructor. I taught English to a small group of Japanese students on Mondays. Luís generally rose late and spent time arranging the center's reading room. Brazilians who were returning to Brazil or moving to other parts of Japan had donated Brazilian magazines, Portuguese language newspapers published in Japan, and a small but growing number of books that accumulated in disorderly

---

[10] The majority of Japanese Brazilians were at least nominally Catholic, and the Japanese Brazilian Catholic priest attracted a large congregation. In addition, groups of Brazilians met sometimes with Japanese congregations of Seichō no Ie, Sōka Gakkai, Mahikari, Tenri-kyō, PL (Perfect Liberation) Kyōdan, Reiyūkai, MOA (Mokichi Okada Association), Mormons, and Jehovah's Witnesses (see Ishi 1995 and Higuchi 1998 for an overview of the followings these groups have attracted among Brazilians in Japan). Among these groups, Seichō no Ie appears to have the most Brazilians members in Hamamatsu. On Japanese religions in Brazil, see Maeyama (1983, 1997). For information specifically on Seichō no Ie in Brazil, also see Maeyama (1996d, 17–21).

piles in the office. One morning or afternoon every other week, Luís distributed flyers on the sidewalks in front of the Bank of Brazil and a Brazilian restaurant downtown, advertising the courses and activities at the center.

Weekday mornings and afternoons were quiet, but evenings were generally busy with telephone calls. People who had received flyers or seen the center advertised in the newspaper called for more information about classes. Occasionally people called Luís with legal or medical problems. Other callers had recently quit their jobs and were in search of new ones. Luís would often refer these cases to the volunteer group Hamamatsu Overseas Laborers Solidarity (HLS) or to the government-administrated Hamamatsu International Communication and Exchange or to brokers who had reasonable reputations. He spent a lot of his telephone time chatting with the instructors, making sure they would be there the following weekend, and suggesting new classes they could consider teaching.

Because many Brazilians in the factories worked every other Saturday, almost all classes were held on Sundays. But the weekend feeling at the center began when the keyboard and chorus teacher, Rosane, showed up on Saturday afternoon. She lived in Yokohama, a two-hour ride by bullet train, and worked part-time during the week for a Portuguese language karaoke journal.[11] Every month, this glossy journal carried stories about Japanese pop stars, along with the romanized lyrics of Japanese songs with their Portuguese translations. Rosane's classes were quite popular and students waiting for their lessons often filled the small living room. She was just twenty years old when she started teaching at the center but had a confident style of teaching to go along with her natural grace and sweet smile. Many students enrolled in more than one of her classes.

The guitar instructor, Carlos, was technically proficient but had an unfortunate predilection for heavy metal. His classes started early Sunday morning, and for most of an hour, he would have his students repeat a single musical phrase over and over. Combined with his gaunt features, deadpan expression, and straight, limp black hair, Carlos's uninspiring teaching limited him for a long time to just a handful of students. This concerned Luís, especially after the Brazilian food and clothing store started offering guitar classes with a more charismatic instructor. Over the course of a year, however, Carlos's teaching improved and he gradually increased his enrollment. In fact, his classes became one of the center's most regular offerings. Other teachers came and went, but Carlos was a constant.

The three dance instructors used a large second-floor room for their

[11] Karaoke ("empty orchestra") has become wildly popular throughout East Asia in the past twenty years. See Hosokawa (1995) for a fascinating account of karaoke culture among Nikkeijin in Brazil.

classes. Although spacious for a tatami room—about forty-five mats—the room was small for a Latin dance studio. In addition, there was no wall mirror, and the lack of air-conditioning made it insufferably hot in August. During one class, someone opened the windows during class, spilling samba and lambada onto the Sunday morning neighborhood. Luís was considering remodeling the third floor to create one large, open space and installing air-conditioning, a full-length wall mirror, and a proper dance floor in place of the tatami. He was also negotiating with an American who owned a combination dance studio and fitness club two blocks away about renting space on weekends.

Andreia taught the samba class and helped with the lambada and jazz dance classes. Andreia was a professional, having graduated from a dance academy in Brazil. She had studied in Spain and Italy as well. She was energetic, and delivered a great pep talk to her students. She was of African and European descent, but had been able to get a visa to work in Japan since her husband was a Nikkeijin. Andreia's charismatic personality and professional training made her class one of the most popular at the center, drawing Japanese as well as Brazilian students. At one point, even the landlord, Sato, enrolled in Andreia's samba class. Working some of the stiffness out of Sato's body was a source of continual amusement and frustration for Andreia. Sato had a classic case of what Gilberto Honda amusingly termed *inhibição pelvica* (pelvic inhibition). Gilberto taught a class on bio-dance, a New Age style of dance that emphasized unblocking the nodes of energy in the body and connecting with a larger cosmic flow. We laughed about Sato's pelvic inhibition, but Gilberto regarded it as a truly pathological condition that afflicted almost all Japanese and many Brazilians working in Japan, the result of social pressures and the stresses of work. Samba dancing involves fast footwork, plus a continuous swiveling of the hips and counterbalancing movement of the shoulders that has the effect of producing a liquid movement in the torso. Sato's hips seemed fused to his spine, his torso rigid and capable only of sudden, unpredictable, jerking motions.

The second-floor sushi bar was staffed by Maria, the wife of the guitar instructor, Carlos. She was selling *pastel* (egg roll skins folded in half rather than rolled, filled with cheese, ham, and other ingredients, and then deep-fried), which she had prepared at home and fried behind the sushi bar. She also sold cans of Guaraná, a Brazilian soft drink with extract of the Amazonian berrylike guaraná fruit. Like samba and coffee, this soft drink had been imported to Japan many years before the "return" migration of Nikkeijin and was sold in cans and bottles by Japanese firms.

In the afternoon, a group of about seven or eight Brazilian women studied *oshibana* (pressed flowers) on the third floor with Mitsuko-sensei (teacher Mitsuko), a Japanese woman in her forties. Oshibana is a relatively new art form although it derives from other decorative crafts with longer traditions. Pressed flowers, stems, and leaves are arranged on stiff paper backing and are affixed with a clear film pressed down on the arrangement. Beginning students started with small rectangular bookmarks; more advanced students moved on to larger arrangements to be framed and hung on walls. Several of Mitsuko-sensei's elaborate works adorned the walls of the center's living room.

Relations with Japanese Neighbors

Japanese landlords were generally reluctant to rent apartments to Brazilians and other foreigners. Sato rented about fifteen apartments to Brazilians, in addition to the properties he rented to Brazilian businesses and organizations such as the Brazilian food and clothing store, the Banco do Brasil, and the culture center. He said that he was very careful about renting to Brazilians, and that he often interviewed them up to four times before agreeing to do so. When I asked him what criteria he used to decide whether to rent to a Brazilian, he replied that knowledge of and compliance with Japanese rules were essential. The Brazilians didn't necessarily have to be able to speak Japanese well as long as they complied with the rules. When I asked him what these rules were, the first thing that he thought of was timeliness in paying the rent. Another Japanese real-estate agent told me that foreigners often did not take their shoes off at the entrance of Japanese apartments. Walking with shoes over tatami mats damages them. Others mentioned that foreigners tended to gather late at night and to make a commotion. Sato said that he was a good judge of Brazilian character, and that he didn't rent to people he thought were likely to have parties. He accepted only quiet, serious types.

Luís took pains to abide by all the written and unwritten rules of residence and tenancy, to cultivate amicable relations with his Japanese neighbors, and to do everything he could not to lose Sato's confidence. He was well aware that his Japanese neighbors would scrutinize him carefully. Despite everything, however, Luís could not avoid certain situations from time to time that led to anonymous complaints to his landlord. For example, one Monday morning after a particularly lively dance class on Sunday, Sato reported to Luís that several neighbors had complained about the noise. Luís was obliged to make a round of apologies to the neighboring houses.

Another source of occasional conflict with neighbors involved the use of a small parking lot across the street from the center; Luís rented one space in the lot each month. On Sundays, the center's guitar teacher had priority use of that space, but invariably a few other visitors would park their cars on the edges of the lot. One of the older women who lived in a house adjoining the lot made it a personal project to survey the lot for infractions and would yell at anyone who left a car there for even a few minutes. We suspected she had made several of the calls about the noise as well. This woman greatly annoyed Luís, but he did his best to remain cordial and to have his Brazilian visitors find parking somewhere else.

One of the most persistent criticisms Japanese had of Brazilian residents was that they did not properly separate their trash for disposal. Luís managed this detail without incident. The rules for sorting garbage were quite complicated in many Japanese cities. The three broadest categories in Hamamatsu were burnable *(moeru gomi)*, non-burnable *(moenai gomi)*, and recyclable. Certain types of plastics were burnable, others non-burnable, and still others recyclable. Most glass bottles were recyclable but had to be separated according to the color of the glass—brown, green, and clear. Aluminum cans and tin cans had to be thrown into different recycling bins. The pickup schedules for the major categories of garbage were different. Burnable items were picked up two or three times per week, non-burnable items just once a week, and recyclables once every other week or so. Foreigners sometimes had trouble complying, and the city later provided a Portuguese translation of the garbage regulations. Luís took pride in his knowledge of the garbage separation details, which had recently gotten even more complex. I knew a Japanese college student who had not figured out what days of the week or month bottles were collected. One corner of his small apartment gradually filled with the recyclable plastic soda bottles he didn't know how to get rid of. Even some of the older Japanese women in the neighborhood expressed frustration with the complexity of the new regulations.

The small group of households near the culture center shared a garbage drop-off point and rotated the responsibility of sweeping the site. Luís carried out this obligation just like everyone else. He also paid the small annual dues to the neighborhood association. A woman who lived with her family next door to us brought him the neighborhood association clipboard with local announcements *(kairanban)*, and advised Luís about many of the ins and outs of the neighborhood and the responsibilities of its residents.

Although Sato and other Japanese often criticized foreigners who disregarded "the rules" of Japanese society, some Brazilians criticized their compatriots for the same reason. Brazilians like Luís, who made a great effort to sort the garbage, minimize noise, and maintain amicable relations with his neighbors, were critical of those who did not make the same effort. But Luís rejected the notion that late-night carousing and noise-making represented a cultural difference between Japanese and Brazilians. When one Japanese acquaintance of mine suggested as much, Luís disputed the remark. He ex-

[107]

plained that Brazilians in Japan often gathered at each other's homes to pass time because they either did not want to spend too much money to go out or did not feel welcome in many public places dominated by Japanese. He disagreed that making noise was culturally acceptable in Brazil and noted that neighbors there often complained about it just as Japanese did.

Luís also rejected the idea that Brazilian culture made it impossible for Brazilians to learn the rules of Japanese society. He was also somewhat impatient with Brazilian complaints about discriminatory practices they faced in Japan. He listened to Brazilians who told him stories about the discrimination they faced in trying to rent apartments, cars, and rooms in hotels, and gave them what advice he could. Afterward, however, he would describe those stories to me as *papo de coitado* (self-pitying talk). He said Brazilians were wrong to accuse Japanese of discrimination without admitting that their own lack of respect for Japanese sensibilities often invited such treatment. Luís's contrarian positions sometimes angered other Brazilians.

Luís was not the only Brazilian to make this sort of critique, however. Those who had been in Japan for years and had made efforts to learn the language and the social conventions where they lived and worked often did not accept the complaints of more recent arrivals about Japanese discrimination. Angelo Ishi has taken fellow Brazilians to task for precisely this reason. He has suggested that "however much a Brazilian swears that he has been discriminated against by a Japanese, it is difficult to know if the Japanese truly had the intention to do so. . . ." (Ishi 1994, 43). He described rumors that had been spread among Brazilians and in the Portuguese language press contending that several shops and a disco in Hamamatsu had barred Brazilians from entry. Ishi investigated by visiting the accused establishments, but found that none of them had such a policy in effect. If any of them had previously excluded Brazilians, they had quickly rescinded the policy. Ishi concluded that the stories that circulated among Brazilians about the discrimination they faced in Japan were greatly exaggerated. In a similar vein, Takeyuki Tsuda, a Japanese American researcher, argues that Nikkeijin generally failed to distinguish between prejudice (which involves attitudes and which does not necessarily involve actions with material consequences) and discrimination (which does involve such actions). Tsuda suggests that Brazilians' frequent claims of discrimination represented their sense of alienation more than actual experiences of discrimination (Tsuda 1998). These studies are far from conclusive, however, especially in light of a 1999 ruling in favor of a Brazilian in a discrimination suit in Hamamatsu (*New York Times*, November 15, 1999; *Daily Yomiuri*, October 13, 1999). A more productive area of study might be long-term residents' chastisement of recent migrants for not living up to the standards the long-term residents have set for themselves.

In fact, Ishi pointed to the fault lines that appeared between long-term and more recent Brazilian migrants to Japan. He suggested that the Brazilian community was coming apart, and that some of the main fault lines appeared between (1) those who intended to live in Japan a significant amount of time and those who intended to return shortly to Brazil, (2) those who were concerned about the public image of Japanese Brazilians and those who were not, (3) those who got along well with Japanese and those who did not, and (4) those who put effort into studying the local language and culture and those who did not (Ishi 1994, 45–46). On the surface, it would seem that those who intended to stay in Japan would most likely also have been the ones concerned with their public image, who got along with Japanese, and who studied the language and culture. Once again, however, this was not necessarily the case.

Luís's critique of Brazilian indifference toward Japanese rules did not mean he supported conformism and assimilation. The courses that the center offered illustrated that he wanted to promote in Brazilians pride and understanding of Brazilian culture, as well as respect and appreciation for Japanese culture. Although Luís was prone to expressing contrarian opinions that could be interpreted as support for assimilation, the center emphasized a Brazilian, more than a Japanese, identity. The care that Luís put into maintaining good relationships with his landlord and neighbors was essential to the existence of the center. Ishi assumed that a Brazilian community, formerly characterized by solidarity, was coming apart as some Brazilian opted to assimilate into Japanese society. He did not allow for the possibility that some Brazilians who enjoyed life in Japan were fashioning themselves as a distinct and visible ethnic minority rather than an assimilated one.

The Culture of Paternalism

The building used for the culture center had been unoccupied for years before Sato rented it to Luís for just 70,000 yen (roughly $700 at the time) per month—the price an average one-bedroom apartment might have cost in Hamamatsu. Even with rusty water pipes, this was fantastic deal for the imposing three-story building. Sato was not running a charity, however. As a businessman, he wanted to rent his properties for a profit. Sato intended eventually to increase the rent to 200,000.

Luís also had to support his living expenses. Luckily he was not a drinker and rarely had the urge to go out at night. He spent nothing on clothing. He was able to arrange free advertising for the center in one of the weekly Portuguese newspapers, and did a lot of the publicity himself. The electricity, gas, and water bills for the center added up to an additional 70,000 to

120,000 yen per month ($700 to $1,200), depending on the season. Moreover, telephone bills ran up to 100,000 yen ($1,000) per month. The base charge on Luís's cellular phone alone was about 20,000 yen ($200). One reason the bills were so high was that he let some of his teachers make long-distance calls. He was especially loose with the chorus and keyboard instructor, Rosane, who would often spend an hour at a time talking with her boyfriend in Nagano Prefecture and sometimes as long talking with friends and family in Brazil.

While the expenditures necessary for maintaining the center were relentless, the income was irregular. Luís was supposed to have taken a percentage of each instructor's earnings to help with expenses, but as I found out much later, the amount he collected depended on the individual instructor's willingness to pay. Like Sato, who charged low rent with the intention of increasing it when the center established a larger following, Luís wanted to foster his instructors, many of whom were just starting out and did not bring students with them. Unfortunately, after asking little financially from the instructors initially, Luís did not have the backbone necessary to get them to pay more when their classes enlarged.

Rosane was a particularly costly investment since Luís had to pay for her train fare to and from Yokohama—14,000 yen ($140) round-trip every weekend—to get her to teach at the center. She taught a few students in the early evening on Saturday, stayed overnight, and taught the rest of her students all day Sunday. Each of her roughly twenty students paid 5,000 yen ($50) per month for her class. She was grossing about 100,000 yen ($1,000) per month, of which Luís asked for 20 percent. Luís paid 42,000 yen per month for Rosane's train fare (she taught only three weekends per month in Hamamatsu) but charged only 20,000 from her income. He did not ask her for enough to cover her train fare and lodging since she was a charismatic figure who attracted people to the center. It was good publicity for the center when she led her chorus in occasional performances or when she placed her individual students in one of the frequent karaoke competitions Brazilians held in different parts of Japan. She also brought students to the center who ended up taking multiple classes. If they were enrolled in chorus, they sometimes also took up dance, guitar, Japanese, English, or oshibana. But Luís was not only unable to have Rosane pay extra; he also was unable to make her pay what he had asked of her.

He eventually had to demand a greater contribution from his instructors, but for a long period Luís paid the center's monthly deficits himself by engaging in a number of sideline businesses. He became a vendor for one long-distance telephone company, an arrangement in which he received a commission for each person he registered for service. He also sold French cosmetics and health products. By supporting the center in this way, Luís fostered the "culture of paternalism," in which certain instructors at the center became accustomed to paying almost nothing for use of the space and resisted his feeble attempts at bill collection. This came to a head when the landlord eventually decided to increase the rent.

The first step Sato took was to let a friend of his start a Brazilian boxed-lunch *(obentō)* business in the sushi bar area. Sato said the friend was willing to pay 50,000 yen per month for the space. Of this, 30,000 would go to Luís—in effect reducing his rent from 70,000 to just 40,000—and 20,000 would go to Sato. Luís was reluctant to give up so much space, but there was little he could say about the matter. He did not have a formal lease from Sato. The obentō business eventually took over most of the second floor. The Japanese owner, Kentaro, and his Brazilian workers installed several refrigerators and freezers, and put a lot of work into cleaning the bar area so that it would pass inspection. He also had a lighting business and installed free of charge several bright fluorescent lighting fixtures for the dim first-floor kitchen and living room as a gesture of good will toward Luís. Luís was always suspicious of Kentaro because of his close association with a disreputable Brazilian disco manager, and he suspected that Kentaro was connected to underworld organizations.

The obentō business eventually made about 150 lunches a day which were delivered by minivan to several factories around town. With their generous portions of meat and almost no vegetables, I found these lunches very heavy, but according to the chief Brazilian cook, light Japanese lunches could not sustain Brazilians working in factories. Only the meat, beans, and rice could provide them with the energy and strength they needed to get through the long workday.

Although Sato expressed confidence in the new business, run by a Japanese manager, discontent among the Brazilian staff and the group's inability to increase sales eventually led to closure of the business. When I revisited the center a year later, I found that the obentō manager had abandoned all of the equipment he had installed, and that a maker of Brazilian pastel had moved in.

Financial Crisis and Conflict

As I was preparing to return to the United States in the spring of 1996, Luís began making plans for what he claimed was the first large-scale celebration in Japan of Brazilian independence day—the Sête de Setembro (September 7). Later in the year, I received in the mail a videotape of the event. It had taken the form of a variety show, including a choral recital, karaoke contest, several theatrical skits, and dance performances. The centerpiece of the festival was a performance choreographed by Gilberto for the students in his bio-dance class at the culture center. The piece started out with carefree figures dancing with smooth, flowing motions across the stage. These figures were conscripted to work in a factory, and their bodies were transformed into machines constantly repeating the same rigid motions, overseen by an arrogant, cigar-smoking, top-hatted caricature of a nineteenth-century American industrialist. In the end, however, the figures broke free and their bodies returned to the swaying natural rhythms, arranged in a harmonious circle.

The all-day independence day program was held in a large auditorium in the center of the city, next to the main train station, and drew an audience of nearly 1,000 people. It was a triumph for Luís and all of the teachers and students of the center, and a testament to the creative spirit and sense of community that the center had fostered. Although many Japanese considered the lives of foreign workers to be completely determined by "necessity," the celebration was a positive expression of Brazilian "extravagance" (see Takaki 1989, 66).

The relationships between the instructors and Luís became decidedly cooler after the independence day celebration, however. The celebration helped build the reputations of some of the center's instructors and increase

Dress rehearsal before the Brazilian independence day show. Photo courtesy of Sandra Nishihara

their class sizes, but the center's finances failed to improve as a result. Luís did not have the will to ask his instructors to contribute more to the center, continuing to insulate them from Sato's desire to increase the rent. One casualty of the financial mismanagement was the library project. Funds designated for the purchase of Portuguese language books to develop the center's library were used to rent the space for the festival and to pay the relentless utilities bills at the center.

Continuing financial difficulties and frustration with his instructors eventually pushed Luís to return to factory work after a two-year hiatus. He had resisted such a move as a point of pride, but later he rationalized that factory work could provide him with a much steadier income and greater peace of mind. I found this ironic, for Luís had originally intended the center as a haven for Brazilians who had lost their cultural and spiritual bearings working in Japan. It became clear, however, that no community, including that built around the center, exists beyond the realm of political and economic relationships. Luís had wanted to construct a moral community that transcended contractual or financial relationships, but he did not foresee that this would mean that he would carry the burden of everyone else's financial responsibilities.

In an environment of general landlord mistrust of foreigners, Luís had succeeded in renting an entire building to house the center. He was able to subsidize and to foster the culture classes first by arranging a low rent for the space, and then by covering most other expenses through a variety of sideline businesses. Through his own benevolence, he had shielded the center from financial realities. When Sato decided to increase the rent, however, Luís had no choice but to redistribute some of the burden among everyone at the center.

Rather than start collecting the extra payments himself, Luís offered the job to Antônia Narita, a student in the keyboard class and a member of the chorus. She would also take care of administrative affairs on weekdays while Luís worked in the factory. The pastel maker who had moved into the place of the obentō business on the second floor also needed someone to help with telephone calls and odd jobs. Luís and the pastel maker agreed to each pay half of her monthly salary of 160,000 yen and to provide her with free lodging at the center.

Antônia originally had come to Japan through the arrangement of a broker and worked for a Sony subcontractor, soldering circuit boards. There was no ventilator for the fumes, which gave her headaches all the time and occasionally made her nauseated. After one month she got another job through a different broker; she worked only two months in that job before being transferred to another firm, which wanted only "pure" Nikkeijin who had some command of the language. Antônia's broker sent her and four others to the firm that had made this request. It was in Toyohashi, about thirty minutes west of Hamamatsu by train. She stayed there for almost two years and got along well with her Japanese bosses and Japanese and Brazilian coworkers. She usually worked two hours of overtime every day and made decent money. When Luís offered her the job as the center's secretary, she hesitated.

She mulled it over for a month before finally deciding to work with Luís. She realized that she would be inserting herself into the middle of tense relationships, but she was committed to the philosophy of the center and felt challenged by the task of getting it back on track. When I met her in the summer of 1997, she claimed that by instituting a new policy for telephone usage and enforcing timely payments from residents and instructors, she had eliminated the monthly deficit within two months of starting work at the center. Antônia complained of how thankless her task was, and, not surprisingly, of all the abuse she took from everyone in accomplishing it.

After about six months, however, Antônia's relationship with Luís had deteriorated. She was angry with him for criticizing her over issues such as keeping the library books in order, and she said he did not appreciate all that she had done. In June 1997, Luís announced at a meeting of instructors that he would be stepping down and that Sato would probably want to start charging 200,000 yen for rent starting in August. Almost no one paid their dues in full for June and July. Rosane paid nothing for June and offered to pay only 20,000 for July. She had an outstanding debt of about 50,000. The pastel maker had failed to pay Antônia her salary for several months. His debt to the center and to Antônia was about 200,000.

The relationship between Antônia and Luís became more and more aggravated during the month and a half I spent with them during the summer of 1997. After Luís resigned as administrator, Antônia, her boyfriend, and several of the center's instructors tried to organize a committee to officially take over from Luís. Antônia told me she could not condemn the instructors for their recalcitrance in paying their bills, for Luís himself had created their bad habits.

His inability to ask people to pay was not his only problem, she said. He dressed badly, he had no self-esteem, and no one respected him, she said. When she first took on her job, she attempted to reform not just the center but also Luís himself, she said. Antônia described how she took Luís to department stores and bought him new clothes to take the place of the tattered rags he had brought with him from Brazil and continued to wear. Her anger at him may have made her exaggerate the extent of Luís's former slovenliness, but she succeeded in making Luís appear more professional than he had before. Antônia said she wanted him to develop a new image and to be able to maintain it on his own. She cleaned his clothes for him, for if she didn't, she said, he would go back to his old habits and his new clothes would become like the ones he had formerly worn.

Luís acknowledged that Antônia's work at the center had been critical in getting it out of the red, but said she had mixed up her professional duties and her desire to look after his personal needs. He also said that she should not expect the respect or affection of the teachers because they had to start paying their bills under her regime. She was an administrator, and administrators would always be hated, Luís said. He, on the other hand, was a creator.

After he resigned, Luís accused the new leaders of the center of the very thing he had been accused of: *"Eles estão fazendo negoçios"* ("They are running businesses"). Luís claimed the purity of culture for himself, adding, *"Todos daquele grupo são oportunistas, aproveitoras"* ("Every one of that group is an opportunist"). He did not give his blessing to Antônia and the other instructors who took over the reins, and within two weeks helped draft a proposal for institutionalizing a cooperative association to run the center. This would have freed the center from the whims of an individual leader or clique. It would have distributed responsibility for the center's finances as well as the symbolic capital that came with administrating.

Luís's proposal came too late, however, and was interpreted by Antônia as a last-ditch attempt to hold on to power. Confiding in me her frustration at the chaos that had engulfed the center, Antônia said that when she met Luís, she did not think of him as manipulative or evil. Now she did. Antônia and the other instructors were not able to keep the center together themselves, and it closed several months later.

The Aftermath of Closing

Soon after the center closed, Antônia returned to Brazil for the first time in almost three years. A month later she returned to Japan and found a job in a Hamamatsu factory. Gilberto, who had been planning to move back to Brazil since I had met him two years earlier, also left Japan at this time, but three months later he was back in Hamamatsu, working in another factory. The building that housed the center continued to house the pastel business on the second floor. Rosane, the karaoke and keyboard teacher, opened her own school on the first floor and made the third floor her residence. According to Luís, the fox that lived in the crawl space between the first and second floors had become a family of foxes and continued to live there.

When I left him in 1997 shortly after his resignation, Luís still expressed a strong feeling of commitment to the ideals of the center. He envisioned another center that one day could play a positive political role for foreigners in Japan. He also vowed to stay in Japan to honor what he described as a pact he had made with other foreigners to pursue his cultural and political projects. Soon after his resignation, he also quit his factory job, this time to try his hand as the Hamamatsu branch manager of a Brazilian telemarketing firm. This venture folded after only a few months. Hounded by debt collectors and bad feelings, he left for a factory job on the Sea of Japan coast, but eventually returned to Hamamatsu and another factory job.

In making a case for the concept of "social drama," Victor Turner has argued that "disturbances of the regular and normal often give us greater insight into the normal than does direct study" (Turner 1974, 34). Although it is tempting to explain the center's dissolution as the result of an insufficient sense of community among Brazilians, I suggest that the "normal" state of affairs at the center was a culture of paternalism that in fact accorded with Japanese ideals of community. The weakness of Luís's personality allowed the center's instructors to take advantage of his patronage without feeling a strong enough sense of reciprocity regarding the financial burden. When financial pressures forced Luís to violate the relationship he had created, the instructors rebelled, much as Japanese workers in the past have protested violations of what they considered the obligations of a paternal management (see Gordon 1985, Smith 1988).

The "normal" state of affairs that the drama of the culture center revealed also included structural constraints that limited Brazilians' ability to rent space, and a discourse that criticized an obsession with money. The structural constraints on foreigners in the housing market kept both Luís and the instructors dependent on the good will of their landlord, Sato. The developing discourse on money obsession informed Luís's ideological separation of the realms of culture and money. The discourse also influenced his failure to recognize that communities exist not only as imagined solidarities, but also as exchange relationships in different degrees of tension with each other. If Luís learned anything from his experiences with the culture center, it may be the importance of developing relationships that from the beginning allow for negotiation and debate rather than foster vulnerable dependencies that collapse with shifting conditions. Indeed, Brazilians' solidarity with each other was much more resiliant than Luís may have imagined.

Despite the mixed feelings that Japanese government officials, business leaders, and workers have expressed with regard to foreign workers, Brazilians have made shaky and tentative steps toward carving a legitimate place for themselves in Japan. For several years, most Brazilians defined their stays in Japan around concrete financial goals. Those who did not proclaim the intention to return to Brazil were assumed to be on the assimilation track, and recent migrants could easily confuse the position expressed by Luís and the editorials of *Nova Visão* toward respect for Japanese rules as a sign of assimilation. It is clear, however, that Luís did not compromise his identity as a Brazilian as he attempted to live in Japan according to Japanese rules. The center promoted pride in Brazilian culture, and its culminating moment was the celebration of Brazilian independence day—according to Luís, the first such event to be held in Japan.

The center has closed, and yet it symbolizes a continuing urge among some Brazilians to express a distinct identity in Japan. Social scientists, company presidents, and government bureaucrats did not see beyond two possibilities: that Brazilians would either assimilate into Japanese society or return to Brazil. They did not foresee a third possibility, that Brazilians would remain in Japan while retaining a strong sense of themselves as Brazilians. It is still too early to say how long Brazilians will continue as a visible ethnic minority in an increasingly multicultural Japan, but it seems clear that they will do so for the time being. And even if they do eventually assimilate to some extent, they will not do so without having some effect on Japanese society. In the next chapter, I explore one Japanese context within which Brazilians were incorporated in a spontaneous manner and which produced surprising syncretic cultural forms.

[6]

Internationalization and the Hamamatsu Kite Festival

Of all the cultural events that occurred throughout the year in Hamamatsu, it was the annual kite festival that natives thought most symbolized local cultural tradition. During the kite festival, foreigners generally served as spectators of Japanese performances of cultural distinction. As such, the festival was not the focus of official efforts to integrate foreign residents into the local community. Yet within the context of the festival, I witnessed the spontaneous production of new syncretic cultural forms arising from Brazilian as well as Japanese sources, and I glimpsed the possibility of integration of a very different sort from that promoted through official internationalization (*kokusaika*) campaigns.

The kite festival centered on the celebration of firstborn sons. Every year, several hundred Hamamatsu families would celebrate their firstborn sons by commissioning their neighborhood associations (*chōnaikai*) to raise kites in their honor. Hundreds of oversized kites (often up to 10 feet long on each side), painted with colorful neighborhood insignia, family crests, and boys' names, were flown over Hamamatsu's ocean dunes for the three days of the festival culminating on Children's Day (*kodomo no hi*), May 5.[1] In the evenings, children seated in ornately carved wooden floats played instruments while being pulled by local residents through neighborhood streets.

---

[1] March 5 is a national holiday based on one of the old bimonthly festivals of Chinese origin; in Japan it has been a day to celebrate little boys. March 3 corresponds to the traditional *Hina matsuri*, the doll festival in honor of little girls, but is not a national holiday. Perhaps out of a desire for relative equality, the national holiday on May 5 was given a gender-neutral name.

The origins of the festival can be traced back to the sixteenth century. The Tourism and Convention Bureau's official guide to the kite festival states:

> The Hamamatsu Festival had its beginnings around 430 years ago. During the period known as the Eiroku Years, from 1558–1569, Iiwo-Buzen-no-Kami, the lord of Hamamatsu Castle . . . celebrated the birth of a son by painting the characters of his son's name on a large kite and boosting it aloft. The idea apparently came from Jingoro Sahashi, a local resident, and sparked a tradition that has continued through the ages. (Hamamatsu-shi Kankō Konbensyon-ka 1996, 4)

This historical narrative is based on the Hamamatsu Castle Records. Yet these records actually contain several more references to Jingoro Sahashi,[2] the putative founder of the festival, which the authors of the official festival guide chose to ignore. The additional references mention that at a certain time, Sahashi made himself a Korean subject (*Chōsen ni kikashite*) and lived in Korea for many years. He eventually returned to Japan as a member of a diplomatic mission and supposedly laughed derisively at Hamamatsu's kites when the mission passed through his old hometown (Yoneda 1986, 2).

Yoneda Kazuo has called into question the validity of the Hamamatsu Castle Records and the identity of the Japanese member of the Korean diplomatic mission as the founder of the kite festival (ibid.). Yet it is significant that at an earlier time, the narrative of the kite festival's origins included a founder who became Korean. In the eighteenth and nineteenth centuries, when some of the dubious entries were made in the Hamamatsu Records, the festival epitomized neither local nor Japanese national traditions, as it came to do in the twentieth century. The current guide excludes any mention of Sahashi's travel to Korea, for such a story would subtly undermine the festival's current role as an emblem of Hamamatsu and Japanese tradition.

For more than three hundred years after Sahashi flew his kite, people and neighborhood groups in the Hamamatsu region flew kites spontaneously, without much coordinated effort. It was not until the early twentieth century that fixed dates and official festival grounds were agreed on, and not until 1917 that the festival achieved its annual continuity, broken only during the war years from 1937 through 1946. During this ten-year hiatus, the only time kites were flown was in 1940, on the 2,600th anniversary of the mythical founding of Japan by the emperor Jimmu.

---

[2] I have retained the English ordering of this name to be consistent with the festival guide's translation. In Japanese, Sahashi, the family name, precedes Jingoro. In addition, Yoneda (1986) notes that the actual pronunciation of the family name is Sabashi rather than Sahashi.

[119]

Rural to urban migration and the incorporation of neighboring townships into an expanding municipality more than doubled Hamamatsu's population in the fifty years after World War II. After the war, in 1947, the festival resumed with thirty participating neighborhood organizations. In 1950, the city government designated it the city's official festival, and within five years the number of participating neighborhoods more than doubled, to sixty-seven. After this initial spurt, few new neighborhoods joined until the early 1980s. Between 1983 and 1996, ninety-one more neighborhoods joined the festival, bringing the total to 158 (Hamamatsu-shi Kankō Konbenshon-ka 1996, 78–79). In 1997, 164 neighborhoods participated.

By incorporating new neighborhoods into the festival, the city has been able to promote a broader consciousness of city membership while strengthening neighborhood solidarity. But to what extent could the festival also incorporate Hamamatsu's newest newcomers, the large numbers of Nikkeijin and other foreign workers? Many Brazilians took advantage of "Golden Week"—the week of national holidays in early May that included the kite festival—to visit friends or just to travel to other parts of Japan. Marginalized within the community of the workplace (chapters 3 and 4) and denied full incorporation by the welfare structure of the national and local governments, Brazilians had formed their own social enclaves such as that surrounding the culture center (chapter 5). Few desired to participate in a festival that was coded as both distinctly Japanese and local. In the context of this Japanese festival *(matsuri)*, however, Japanese and Brazilians created an enthusiastic syncretic cultural form and pointed to the possibility of Nikkeijin incorporation into the neighborhood and citywide communities.

The Japanese term *matsuri* is linked to the Japanese verbs *matsurau* and *matsuru*, which John Nelson defines respectively as "attending to" a deity and "venerating or enshrining" (1996, 39). Matsuri generally involve rapport with a sacred and spiritual realm, centering on a local shrine and its deity. The Hamamatsu Festival (Hamamatsu Matsuri) shares many of the elements of other Japanese festivals but is peculiar in that it does not involve any shrine or deity. Whether festivals and rituals involve the transcendental realm, however, they generally function to "suspend everyday routine" (DaMatta 1991, 28). In Hamamatsu's suspension of everyday routine, Brazilian culture was incorporated into Japanese activity in a way I had not seen in other contexts.

Like Jingoro Sahashi, who left Japan for Korea and returned many years later, Japanese in the past century left for Brazil and other Latin American countries, and second- and third-generation Japanese Brazilians have plotted the reverse course toward Japan. Few official efforts have been made to incorporate Japanese Brazilians into the festival. The spontaneous incorporation of Brazilian culture within the framework of the festival, however, holds out the possibility for a greater integration of peoples and an acceptance of modern Sahashis who have traveled far and returned. The cultural syncretism was especially significant in that it involved Japanese blue collar workers, who, as chapters 3 and 4 illustrate, appeared to be ambivalent if not hostile toward Nikkeijin.

Kite Flying and Neighborhood Solidarity

In recent years, the festival has included three major activities: kite flying, processions of wooden floats, and nighttime parties in front of the houses of firstborn sons and sponsors. In the mornings and afternoons, all neighborhoods would gather by the beach to fly kites. In the evenings of the first and third days of the festival, most of the neighborhood associations that had a wooden float held processions through their own neighborhoods. The second evening, all wooden floats were brought to the center of the city to join in a group procession. Costing several hundred thousand dollars each, these wooden floats were prohibitively expensive for many neighborhoods. In 1996, of the 158 neighborhoods that participated in the kite-flying part of the festival, only eighty owned wooden floats.

Each night after dark, neighborhoods had their own self-contained succession of parties in front of the houses of families that had firstborn sons in the previous year. Owners of neighborhood shops and other businesses also sponsored parties in front of their establishments. Sponsorship of kites and parties was costly. The price of a kite depended on its size, measured in tatami mat units. An acquaintance of mine who had celebrated the birth of a son by sponsoring a kite the previous year said that one tatami unit costs about 45,000 yen ($450). Thus, the six-tatami kite he sponsored for his son cost about 270,000 yen ($2,700). All told, he estimated the expenses he had incurred by celebrating his son the previous year totaled almost 700,000 yen ($7,000). Besides the cost of the kite itself, the major expense was all the food and drink that he had to provide for the party in front of his house. In his neighborhood, eleven families had sponsored both kites and parties, and another ten had sponsored only parties. Possibly another twenty or so families did not participate at all. People living in apartments faced no pressure to participate, he said. Although he claimed that he too had not been pressured into sponsorship, as the owner of a neighborhood noodle shop he no doubt considered full participation in the festival a wise investment.

The elaborately carved wooden floats, which residents pulled around their neighborhoods, served a similar purpose as the portable shrines (*mikoshi*) of other Japanese festivals that people carried on their shoulders to mark neighborhood locations and boundaries (see Bestor 1992, Ashke-

[121]

nazi 1993, Schnell 1999). Yet unlike the portable shrines, the floats were not infused by the spirit of the local deity. These floats were known as palace carts *(goten yatai)* and had the double- or triple-layered roofs characteristic of medieval Japanese castles.

From 1919 through 1966 (not including the wartime hiatus), the festival was held on the grounds of the 67th Infantry Division stationed in Hamamatsu not far from the city center (Koike 1981, 42–43). The festival moved to the beachside grounds after outgrowing its old home. Starting in 1967, kites were flown on a large sandy clearing the size of four or five football fields among pine groves by the beach. Every day of the festival in 1994 and 1995, the kite-flying grounds were filled with thousands of men in festival garb, roughly thirty to a neighborhood, running in all directions. Each participating neighborhood had a distinct insignia that decorated the backs of the *happi*, the wide-sleeved jackets tied with sashes that are worn during festivals in many parts of Japan. Neighborhood groups painted the same insignia boldly on the kites that they flew so that they were easily identifiable from a distance. Thousands of spectators strained to get dramatic photos while dodging rushing teams of kite flyers and their frequently crashing kites. The grounds were filled with shouts and dust, and the skies were filled with huge kites. New kites were usually flown in the mornings, the afternoons being given over to older ones. Each neighborhood had ten or more kites of various sizes. Smaller kites were used when it was windy. Larger ones were more effective when the breeze was light. Most neighborhoods used a character from their neighborhood names as the central motifs for their insignia. When every neighborhood had a kite aloft, the sky became a haphazard and shifting representation of the neighborhood organization that existed on the ground in Hamamatsu. Neighborhood identity had greatest significance for members of the old middle class, the shopkeepers and small manufacturers who dominate many neighborhood associations (see Bestor 1989, 1992), and the blue-collar residents who associated with them. Many people however, had crosscutting relationships with several neighborhoods, and some of them may not have normally thought of their neighborhood as a unit of identification at all; during the festival, however, the kites established neighborhoods as the fundamental unit of organization and identification.

Bugle players in each neighborhood roused the ranks to action when kites were flown in battle and their lines were deliberately entangled. Each team tried to sever the lines of opponents' kites by using friction. Physical strength was an important asset for any kite-flying group when up to six converging groups tugged and heaved in unison on their own hemp lines, until one by one the lines would wear through, sending kites crashing gracefully into the pine trees or onto the dunes or blowing out to sea. Un-

Kites with distinctive neighborhood designs fill the sky

like participants in the Nagasaki kite festival, participants in the Hama-matsu festival did not implant shards of glass in the lines. Groups tried to distribute the friction over their line to prevent it from wearing through by occasionally releasing their grips and letting the kite pull more line out. There was a lot of rough elbowing and shouting among the groups of men who were pulling on their lines next to each other, and scuffles sometimes ensued. These were limited, however, because of sanctions enforced by the festival organizers.

Ishida, a man about forty years old, usually took charge of much of the kite flying in the neighborhood with which I participated. During the festival itself, it was crucial to get a kite off the ground without entangling it with other kites rising all around it. This was especially important when raising the new kites sponsored by families of firstborn sons. The baby's entire family would gather on the flying grounds and observe anxiously as their kite was lifted into the sky. Ishida, boasting that he was the best in the neighborhood, would generally monopolize the kite flying. Two or three other men would hold the kite about twenty-five yards downwind from Ishida, and, at his signal, would push the kite aloft as he ran backward. Ishida would yank the line to the ground three or four times using his whole body, run back some more, and repeat these actions so that the kite rose in a series of upward jerks. When it would momentarily sink, the kite's rope tail—five or six yards long—would snake onto the ground, sometimes curling around

A firstborn son looking on with parents as neighborhood men fly his kite

people's legs, then would slither and whip upward as Ishida ran and tugged on the line, lifting the kite higher into the sky. Sometimes winds would cause the kite to writhe to the left and then to the right, its tail swishing back and forth until it got caught on another kite. No longer stabilized by its tail, the kite would plunge toward the ground, pulling down any kite with a line in the path of descent. Accusations of incompetence would fly between neighborhood groups. Falling kites also led to many head injuries during the festival, with some of the men wearing bandages and streaks of blood as badges of honor.

The scene, with men scrambling in all directions, banners waving, and people shouting excitedly, resembled images of a medieval Japanese battle-field. The insignia of the kites flying overhead proclaimed neighborhood identities. The entanglement of kite lines underscored the sometimes only barely controlled roughhousing between members of different neighbor-hoods. The community represented in the kite festival was one constituted in tension among warring neighborhoods. But as such, the festival served as a symbol of Hamamatsu. As one long-term participant in the festival and lifelong employee at one of the major car manufacturers said, the competi-tive and boisterous quality of Hamamatsu residents expressed itself both in the kite festival and in the fierce competition among local firms that have made many of them internationally successful.

Native Place-making and Internationalization

An aura of tradition surrounds many of Japan's festivals, even those such as Hamamatsu's which have taken their current form relatively recently. Jennifer Robertson has written about the role of festivals as a part of a broad movement known as *furusato-zukuri* (native place-making), which pro-moted tourism by casting towns as the repositories of traditions that were disappearing from modern, urban Japan (Robertson 1991, chapter 2). Townships reconstructed thatched-roof farmhouses and castles as part of their native place-making programs to promote tourism. They reinvigorated festivals, and promoted local handicrafts and culinary specialties. All of these projects conjured timeless traditions and lifestyles for urban dwellers who felt a distance between themselves and the countryside. Robertson writes that "the sheer ubiquity of such programs . . . work[s] to insure that nostalgia becomes a natural(ized) frame of mind shaping desires and moti-vating patterns of consumption" (ibid., 105).

Festivals appear unlikely contexts in which to find examples of interna-tionalization, for tradition looks backward toward some notion of an au-thentic and singular Japan, while internationalization looks toward a multicultural future. Internationalization *(kokusaika)* discourse swept through the Japanese media in the 1980s and 1990s. For many, it offered the possibility of opening up and stimulating what appeared to be a closed and stagnant society. Yet Robertson has noted that a "shared and willfully nostalgic rationale [underpins] the rhetoric of both native place-making and internationalization" (Robertson 1997, 114). While programs that were dedicated to nostalgic native place-making attempted to re-create a way of life that had grown temporally distant, internationalization programs attempted to re-create cultures that were spatially removed.

The two types of programs resemble each other in their efforts to sanitize and to commercialize the cultural differences that they both apparently embrace. International theme parks have sprung up throughout Japan. Little World in Nagoya celebrates multicultural diversity of architectural forms by reconstructing representative houses from different cultures around the world. Other projects such as the Holland Village Huis Ten Bosch in Nagasaki, the Parque España in Mie Prefecture (Robertson 1997, 101), and the "Danish Town of Kyoto," as Tamba-cho presents itself (Knight 1993, 213), focus on single foreign countries. In the case of Tamba-cho, internationalization and native place-making converge. John Knight notes that rural depopulation has stimulated many towns to search for foreign as well as Japanese historical motifs with which to market the towns as exotic resorts for urban dwellers. The internationalization at the village level is intimately connected to small towns' increasing dependence on a national market for local cultural production (ibid., 214). It is an internationalization that involves marketing the foreign to Japanese tourists.

Robertson's suggestion that internationalization and native place-making share the same underlying nostalgic rationale offers a critical perspective on some of the official forms internationalization has taken. Based on her research in the city of Kodaira, Robertson writes that the Kodaira citizens' festival *(shimin matsuri)* dialectically constituted the city as a community through highlighting the tension between newcomers and natives (Robertson 1991, chapter 2). Kodaira "natives" (those claiming descent from the village founders) retained exclusive rights over the performance of the most dramatic and prestigious parts of their festival, enacting a hierarchical relationship between themselves and more recent Japanese migrants. In a recent update of this festival, however, Robertson notes that since the addition of a foreigners' segment to the festival parade in 1992, the distinction between Japanese and foreigner has displaced the older tension between Japanese natives and newcomers (Robertson 1997, 100–101). The dynamic she describes in transformations of the Kodaira festival is similar to that which I described in the Yusumi factory (chapter 3). There, the presence of foreign workers partially displaced the tension Japanese workers had been feeling toward their managers and their firm, leading Japanese workers to revive a discourse concerning responsibility toward one's firm at a time when many of them had ambivalent feelings toward it.

In the context of the kite festival in Hamamatsu, however, I found that the presence of Brazilians may have reinforced rather than displaced tensions among different groups of Japanese residents. For much of the past century, the pursuit of upward mobility has been associated with movement toward a middle-class lifestyle that idealizes samurai tradition. Many Japanese have been caught up in a race for status as defined by entrance into elite universities, professional status, or stable employment in large, prestigious firms (see Vogel 1971, Kelly 1993). The cultural roots of these new status criteria were in the austere bureaucratic samurai class, which has long been set against another group of Japanese, the colorful premodern merchant class of the *shitamachi* ("low city," referring to old mercantile quarters) (see Smith 1960, Seidensticker 1983).

After a long postwar decline of shitamachi status, the 1980s saw a revalorization of merchant culture tradition. Shitamachi today is associated with "an 'authentic' and distinctly 'traditional' way of life, which has slipped away from most urban Japanese" (Bestor 1993, 57). The shitamachi (mercantile downtown) revival that Bestor discusses shares some of the characteristics of the native place-making movement. Both are infused with nostalgia for more authentic, premodern lifestyles. The difference between them is that the shitamachi model is based on a premodern urbanism, while furusato-zukuri is based more on the opposition between rural and urban lifestyles.

Like Robertson, Marilyn Ivy has argued that regional cultural differences which were at one time threatening to mainstream ideologies are recuperated in highly sanitized and commercialized forms when sociological referents are on the verge of extinction (Ivy 1995). The revival of shitamachi ideals appears to fit Ivy's analysis of "discourses of the vanishing." Although the shitamachi cultural revival has been nostalgically imagined by many members of the upwardly mobile middle class, however, there is a very significant blue-collar contingent in addition to the old middle-class shopkeepers, who "view themselves as the true heirs to the rough-and-tumble lifestyles of pre-modern shitamachi. . . ." (Bestor 1992, 42). Their claims are based much more on opposition to the upwardly mobile (and nostalgic) middle class than on a nostalgia for a lost tradition.

Blue-collar workers are often held to be the most antagonistic to migrants because they compete for the same jobs. Indeed, some Brazilians I interviewed complained about the negative attitudes of their Japanese coworkers, and certain Japanese workers at Yusumi were antagonistic toward foreigners. Many, however, had amicable relations, and I noticed in my neighborhood association that a few Japanese blue-collar workers invited Brazilians, Peruvians, Indians, Thai, and other foreigners with whom they became acquainted at work. By contrast, white-collar workers and their wives tended to invite Europeans and Americans.

Harold Isaacs considers basic group identity to derive from ethnicity, to which other nodes of identification, such as the workplace, school, or age group, are subordinate (Isaacs 1975). Discussing other regions of the world, scholars have described how ethnic and racial identification often trump class solidarity (Bourgois 1989, Comaroff 1987, Saxton 1971, Takaki 1989). In the context of the festival, I found that the status conflict between shita-machi representatives (including shopkeepers and blue-collar workers) and those who identified with a more upwardly mobile new middle class led to two distinctly different ways of incorporating Nikkeijin. Although members of the middle class were eager to promote the festival to foreigners as an example of traditional Japanese culture, blue-collar workers were capable of creating syncretic[3] forms through spontaneous interaction with Nikkeijin and Brazilian cultural elements. The case that follows not only calls into question assumptions of blue-collar antagonism toward foreign workers; it also forces us to acknowledge the possibility that under certain circumstances, solidarity arising from class-coded culture across ethnic lines can be more significant than ethnic solidarity across class lines. It forces us to think more carefully about the interaction of gender, class, ethnic, racial, and national identities.

Inviting Foreign Guests

I was invited by an acquaintance, Yagawa Haruo, to join his neighborhood for the month long preparations leading up to the festival as well as for the festival itself. I had met him at the weekly gatherings of a group called the Hippo Family Club, whose members had the goal of learning numerous foreign languages simultaneously. This group had a distinct philosophy for language acquisition. Its members had rejected the type of English language education that all Japanese must suffer for at least six years in junior and senior high schools and which is almost exclusively directed toward passing the English component of written college entrance exams. They advocated what they called natural language acquisition, through listening and

---

[3] Since I am dealing primarily with a ritual context in this chapter, I prefer to use the term "syncretic" to "hybrid," the former term having a history of usage in religious studies. Also, the combination of elements from Brazilian and Japanese sources I describe did not result in a fundamentally new form at the genetic level (which we would expect in a hybrid form), but rather supplied a new flavor to the Japanese ceremony without changing its underlying structure (as we would expect in a syncretic form) (see Stewart and Shaw 1994).

mimicking, without the use of textbooks and dictionaries. It was an extraordinary group, not only because the members attempted to learn seven languages at the same time just using taped versions of the same story in each language, but also because most of its members were parents of young children, and their meetings were a riot of jubilant children singing, dancing, and running about. For about half the session, the adults joined the children in singing and dancing to a tape of songs in foreign languages, or playing simple games. What was extraordinary was that a significant number of fathers attended these meetings and, after several weeks of embarrassment and refusal, started to take part in the games wholeheartedly.[4]

Yagawa was unusual among the members of this group, joining on his own, without his wife's initiative or participation. He was a rather silent man who did not do very well with the group's language-acquisition technique, and yet he seemed to enjoy the group, especially playing with the children, most of whom were between several months and eight years old. It was a completely different world from the Shimokawa neighborhood association, which he invited me to join for the month long kite festival preparations in April.

Yagawa was always uncomfortable when someone from the neighborhood association asked him how we had met. He would mumble something about English conversation, to which he would get a surprised reaction. Not wanting to embarrass him by describing what went on at the Hippo Family Club, I usually just nodded politely. As it was, many in this neighborhood group thought of English conversation as a somewhat effeminate activity. People occasionally reacted by asking Yagawa for a demonstration of his English language abilities, to which he rarely responded with more than "This is a pen," a phrase that has appeared for a generation on page one of first-year junior high English textbooks in Japan. This demonstration of ineptitude on Yagawa's part seemed to reassure the rest of the neighborhood men that nothing was amiss, that he still was who they thought he was.

Every night for a month prior to the festival, about fifteen men from the neighborhood would straggle into Shimokawa's two-story concrete neighborhood meeting hall (*kōkaido*) at about 7:30 to repair kites damaged in the previous year's festival. One of the key tasks was to remove the tattered old paper from the kites, add new paper, and then paint in any portions of the color scheme and insignia that had been removed. This kind of work went on for at most an hour, inevitably followed by beer drinking and chatting, with TV tuned to a baseball game, usually featuring the Chūnichi Dragons based in Nagoya, the closest major league team.

[4] Many Japanese fathers are distant from their families, especially in the upwardly mobile middle class, where demands of work and company-related recreation are great (see North 1994).

[129]

On the second floor of the hall, children between seven and fourteen years old practiced the festival melodies for bugle and flute. The mothers who accompanied the children stayed on the second floor except when they needed men's advice on important questions. Yagawa had been the leader of the children's committee for several years, and women would go to him rather than the other men to ask questions. Women were almost never invited to join the men in their discussions over beer and snacks on the raised sitting area on the first floor where the men spent most of their time. For the men, these evening gatherings were as much an opportunity to socialize as they were a time to repair kites and to take care of other matters such as deciding what route the float should take through the neighborhood and the order of the nightly street parties. Those who made decisions regarding the float and street parties tried to ensure that the processions would not retrace their steps.[5]

Some evenings, I would have dinner at Yagawa's house before going to the neighborhood hall. Conversation was never very lively unless the rest of his family was also present. He lived with his three children, wife, and her parents. One evening, I asked him whether his parents had dedicated a kite to him when he was born. After a longer silence than I was accustomed to, Yagawa mumbled that he had grown up near Nagoya in Aichi Prefecture to the west. He was an outsider *(yoso no mono)*, compared with those whose families had been in the neighborhood several generations. His status as a "married-in" son-in-law *(muko yōshi)*, combined with his reticence, had affected his status in the kite festival and neighborhood associations. He had been a full participant in festival preparations for more than twenty years, but seemed to be perennially stuck with lower-status roles such as children's committee leader. His love of young children fit him for this role, but in the context of the festival preparations and the masculine ideals of the festival

---

[5] This was also the case when members of the neighborhood association delivered kites to the families of firstborn sons one week before the festival. This avoidance of retracing one's steps recalls the circular routes taken during funeral processions as well as later visits to grave sites; a circular route is intended to confuse the spirit of the deceased, to keep it from following you home. The processions during the kite festival celebrate the start of the life cycle, while funerals mark the end of the life cycle. The avoidance of retracing steps in both cases may indicate a concern with the proper progression of the soul through the states of pre-birth, life, and death. At each house that the neighborhood association group visited when delivering kites before the festival and at night during the festival itself, one of the association leaders would lead the crowd in banzai cheers for the health and robust growth of the firstborn son. William LaFleur writes that the souls of children who died before the age of seven were thought to return to the pre-birth state during the Tokugawa era, when infant and early childhood mortality rates were high (LaFleur 1992). The banzai cheers for the growth and health of the son during the festival, as well as the prohibition on retracing one's steps during processions, promote a forward progression and resist the prospect of early death and regression of the soul from the realm of the living to that of the pre-living, or from death to living.

itself, it carried low status. The only time some of the others had contact with the women and children in the association hall was the night before the first day of the festival when the children put on a short concert. Even then, however, status differences were clearly marked, with men sitting in rows of seats set up on the second floor while the women stood around the edges of the room.

One weekend afternoon, Yagawa invited a man from India, whom he had met through the Hippo Family Club, to visit the neighborhood association hall and to observe the festival preparations. Gupta was in Japan as a technical trainee at Yusumi in conjunction with Yusumi's Indian joint venture. Most of the Japanese at the neighborhood hall that day ignored him as they went about their business. But one neighborhood resident, Kobayashi, turned out to have known Gupta in India from several years previously. Kobayashi had spent three years in India with the joint venture, specializing in quality control. He immediately went into a long discourse about how he had enjoyed his tour of duty in India and what an interesting country it was. On the basis of his experiences, Kobayashi asserted that the caste system was a reason that neighborhood associations like Shimokawa's did not exist there. I could see Gupta stifle a reply as Kobayashi turned to me and asked if neighborhood associations existed in the United States. For Kobayashi, the presence of Gupta and me created an "international" situation in which he could both demonstrate authoritative knowledge of the foreign in front of Japanese acquaintances and turn a routine afternoon of kite preparations into a reflection of the uniqueness of Japanese community organization and festival tradition.

Although no other foreigners were invited to the month long preparations for the festival, several were invited for the festival itself. They were given festival clothing and the chance help pull the float around the neighborhood or to hold the kite line for a minute after the kite was flying at a stable height. One Japanese member of the Shimokawa group jovially referred to a Peruvian guest as *"Mistā Peru."* This guest was of Japanese ancestry, spoke Japanese well, and had lived in Japan for seven years. Nevertheless, in the context of the festival, he was identified by foreign nationality and primarily filled the role of a foreign observer who could confirm the kite festival as a heightened symbol of traditional Japan.

The blue-collar workers at the neighborhood association I joined for the festival preparations had mixed feelings about my presence. I too had mixed feelings—I felt simultaneously refreshed and uncomfortable. It was refreshing not to be confronted with the stylized awe and amazement people often displayed when I was introduced to them as an American from New York, or as a researcher affiliated with Cornell University. By contrast, people in the neighborhood association often acknowledged my presence with only the most informal of glances and grunts. I lent a hand in the month long festival preparations at the neighborhood hall several times each week in April. One evening, drinking sake after applying new paper to old bamboo kite frames, a construction worker in his sixties named Shimizu induced me to think more about internationalization in terms of status and class. The festival brought out things that normally go hidden, he told me, and added that by studying this, I might understand a bit of the character (*kishitsu*) of Hamamatsu. He emphasized that his was an old neighborhood in which the ties of human feeling were thicker (*ninjō ga komayaka*) than in other neighborhoods. Arguments, discord, and bad feelings among neighborhood people during the rest of the year were all put aside during the festival, when everyone was united by a single purpose. Then he told me that he didn't like it when people visited them during festival time just once and disappeared. That kind of relationship was meaningless. I reminded him I had participated the year before and planned to do so again that year, but he just looked at me and said that I did not really understand the essence of the festival and the Japanese spirit, the Hamamatsu spirit.

The festival brought out tensions that some blue-collar residents felt in relation to people they saw as having middle-class pretensions, who paraded a series of foreign guests, primarily high-status North Americans and Europeans, through the neighborhood association on one-shot visits. Shimizu was hostile to these invitations. For other blue-collar workers as well, the festival was not about internationalization at all. It was an opportunity to fraternize with neighbors, drink a lot, celebrate firstborn sons, and demonstrate themselves as the possessors of a specific form of masculinity essential for the festival and tied to Hamamatsu city tradition.

Kite Festival Samba

On each of the three nights of the festival, people in Shimokawa gathered at the neighborhood association hall around nine o'clock. Then, to the sound of drum and whistle in a repetitive "don don, pi pi, don don, pi pi" and the chanting of "*Wa-shoi! Wa-shoi! Wa-shoi! Wa-shoi!*" the group of between one hundred and two hundred young men and women carrying candle-lit paper lanterns walked in the direction of the first house that was sponsoring a celebration with food and drink. As the group approached the house, the rhythm accelerated, and a bugle joined the drums and whistles as the group half marched, half jogged in a circle in front of the entrance, where the household head, family, and friends stood to welcome them. The circle of revelers gradually tightened to form a mass of bodies bobbing up and down and rotating around two flag bearers in the center. Heat and pressure were concentrated in the center, where the flags shook and swayed, pressed in on all sides. The members of the neighborhood association stood along the edges, with both hands raised overhead, urging the revelers on with their chants of "Wa-shoi! Wa-shoi!" A long whistle call signaled the bugle, other whistles, drums, and chanting to stop, and the circle dispersed, only to come rushing together once again when the whistle started blowing the rhythm, quickly taken up again by the other instruments. This pattern of repeated compression and dispersal reflected the festival as a whole, which brought the neighborhood together for a brief period, only for many of its residents to disperse again into their separate routines. The dispersed individuals did not revert to a completely pre-festival state, however, having been infused with the concentrated spirit of the community, which lingered with them in the form of discussions in later weeks about the events and experiences of the festival.

Upon a long whistle call, the circle of bodies unwound for a final time; leaders of the festival council then greeted the hosts of the party and wished prosperity for them and robust growth for their son. The head of household then stood between the flag bearers, put his infant on his shoulders, and was in turn taken onto the shoulders of one of the strongest young men in the festival group. This pillar of masculinity, buttressed by the flag bearers, stood firm as the drums, whistles, and chanting started again and another rotating circle of crushing bodies formed around them. At some houses, the mother would be raised up on another man's shoulders alongside the father and the son, but I never observed the son on his mother's shoulders. Much more often, the mother was not raised up at all, and it was the *patriline* that stood at the center of the communal mass.

Festival rules prohibited children under fifteen from participating in this nighttime reveling. Until the early 1990s, high school students had not been allowed either. I found it hard to imagine the revelry without the high school students, however, since they exuded a sexual energy vital in making the dancing and chanting wheel of bodies a worthy tribute to the hosts of the party.

On the second night of the festival in 1995, I decided to leave Yagawa and the Shimokawa neighborhood to visit a different neighborhood, where a friend was sponsoring a party for his firstborn son. Unlike Shimokawa, this neighborhood was not in the older section of the city and could not claim a long history of participation in the festival. Yet it was similar in that a large proportion of its residents were blue-collar workers. My friend Kimpara Naoto worked in a factory, where he had gotten to know several Brazilians coworkers and developed an interest in samba. That interest led him to join a local samba group composed primarily of Japanese but which included several Brazilian members. He was also an active member of his neighbor-

Pillar of masculinity: firstborn son on father's shoulders; father on neighborhood man's shoulders—all surrounded by a rotating mass of revelers

hood kite festival group. He was only twenty-nine years old in 1995, but had been a member of his neighborhood group since the year after it was formed, about ten years previously. Kimpara's parents were originally from Mie Prefecture, one prefecture beyond Aichi to the west, but perhaps because their neighborhood had a short history of participation in the festival, their neighbors did not stigmatize them as outsiders during the festival. Kimpara told me that several people had had reservations when he proposed including samba during the party that he sponsored in front of his house. In the end, however, the head of his neighborhood association said that because Kimpara was the father of the child, the decision was his. As long as the celebration got people excited (*moriagaru*), as long as it filled them with the festival spirit, there would be no problem. As it turned out, the samba was a huge success.

Seven members of the samba band—four Japanese, two Brazilians, and I—set up our drums at the end of Kimpara's driveway. When we heard the rowdy crowd of neighborhood people heading our way from the previous party, we started banging our drums and blowing our whistles to the simple two-beat rhythm of the revelers. We continued as the crowd formed a tight, frenzied circle revolving in front of us, and stopped when the leader of the festival group blew his whistle. The circle of bodies unwound, and leaders of the festival council greeted the hosts of the party and wished them well.

Japanese and Brazilian members of a local samba group practicing in a wooded park

Kimpara then stood between the flag bearers, put his infant on his shoulders, and was in turn taken onto the shoulders of one of the strongest young men in the festival group. After a couple of minutes, the drumming stopped and the ecstatic wheel unwound and dispersed, people sitting on the street in front of the house, waiting for the food and drinks to be passed around. Twenty minutes later, toasts were made to Kimpara, who was again taken up onto someone's shoulders as the revelers crushed around them, this time circling to the alternating rhythms of samba and the traditional two-beat "don don, pi pi."

This was the third or fourth house that the crowd was visiting and many people were tipsy from all the drinks they had had. Yet the spirit of the festival was even more boisterously and jubilantly expressed at Kimpara's house than alcohol alone normally inspires, at least partially thanks to the much faster syncopated rhythms of samba that we played. The band and the crowd switched back and forth between the two rhythms, each inspiring the other to new heights of enthusiasm. It was an exemplary performance of festival spirit, yet unlike any that people had experienced before. Kimpara's wife and mother, and Kimpara himself, shed tears of joy as the crowd again and again re-formed their circle of crushing bodies, until finally they had to go to the next party, shouted their congratulations, and staggered down the road.

[135]

Writing about rituals in plural societies, Gerd Baumann (1992) suggests we replace the idea of ritual community with that of ritual constituencies. The term "constituency" better expresses the way in which rituals are often performed with "Others" in mind, and often with them present as spectators or guests. To some extent, foreigners were the "Others" for white-collar Japanese at the festival. The "Others" for blue-collar workers, however, turned out to be the ever greater numbers of Japanese who have pursued status through attendance of elite universities and subsequent employment in large, prestigious firms in the postwar era. Blue-collar workers have not "made it" according to these criteria, but the Hamamatsu kite festival and the overall revival of shitamachi ideals have provided them the opportunity to represent themselves as carriers of an "authentic" Japanese spirit.

The incorporation into festival activity of Hamamatsu's newest newcomers—Brazilians and other foreign workers—ultimately may not be as easily achieved as the incorporation of the new bedroom communities has been during the past twenty years. Many Japanese continue to think of foreign residents as temporary rather than permanent, and many may not welcome an internationalization of the festival that involves more than an opportunity to demonstrate Japanese traditions to foreign observers. Internationalization efforts such as the invitations extended to Euro-American tourists by white-collar participants in the festival and the English language guidebook published by the Hamamatsu city government focused attention on the difference between Japanese and foreign. An internationalization that exaggerates national differences does little to incorporate resident foreigners into local society. It may, in fact, ideologically support the exclusion of Nikkeijin and other foreign residents from full membership within workplace communities, which may entail not just slights to their dignity but also denial of important rights such as comprehensive health insurance.

However, the successful syncretism of Brazilian music and Japanese revelry at Kimpara's house demonstrates that Japanese may be able to internationalize in a fashion that avoids reifying notions of Japanese tradition. Blue-collar workers participated in a form of internationalization—the kite festival samba—without threatening their self-portrayal as carriers of an authentic tradition; the excitement of the samba worked within the structure of the festival and emphasized the characteristics that blue-collar workers had already claimed as their own.

The construction worker Shimizu articulated a critique of official internationalization as involving only superficial "one-shot meetings" (*tōri ippen no tsukiai*). We must be willing to question what official internationalization really means, and likewise, we must be willing to consider the possibility of a more meaningful unofficial internationalization on the part of those who are often considered the most reactionary with regards to it. The instance of syncretism of samba and kite festival suggests that blue-collar workers, within certain contexts, may even be more capable than self-proclaimed proponents of internationalization of interacting with foreigners in terms that do not exclusively emphasize national cultural differences. Whereas many Japanese cast foreign workers as lower-class people from impoverished countries and in doing so reinforce their own claims to mainstream status (see Lie 2001, 28–35), Japanese blue-collar workers, whose occupations have also been denigrated, may have been able to develop affinities with foreign workers in opposition to mainstream idealization of stable white-collar employment.

Ritual contexts, however, do not necessarily reflect the dynamics of daily interactions in a direct manner. During festivals, role reversals between rich and poor, master and slave, may just serve to highlight and to reinforce social distinctions maintained during the rest of the year, rather than lead to a more tangible reorganization of social and economic power (see Gluckman 1963, Linger 1992). The *communitas* achieved between Japanese and Brazilians during the kite festival, however, may be significant in that it offers an alternative vision of how these two groups may relate to each other. It is a vision of a mutually enriching relationship rather than one in which one group is forcibly incorporated by another.

Groups and cultural influences have been incorporated into Japanese society and culture in the past, but this has often involved either the erasure or exaggeration of their formal markers of foreignness, either of which would maintain the sense of discrete "Japanese-ness." The Brazilian elements in the syncretic performance of kite festival samba, however, retained a distinct aura of difference even as they exemplified the spirit of the festival. The primary obstacles to such an incorporation of the foreign in wider social contexts may be in the arrangement of political and economic institutions, rather than in a deep-rooted bias against the foreign within Japanese culture. That Brazilians could be incorporated within a festival symbolic of Japanese tradition suggests that foreigners could be more easily incorporated within other contexts.

Finally, we must note that the syncretism of Brazilian and Japanese cultural elements occurred in the context of a highly masculinist festival. We must not celebrate this syncretism without also considering the possibility that it is based not only on class tensions but also on enduring gender inequality. Can Japanese embrace only certain Brazilian cultural elements that accord with Japanese patriarchy? If this instance of cultural syncretism incorporated just one aspect of Brazilian culture, how much does it reveal about the possibility that Japanese institutions and individuals can embrace the full diversity of Nikkeijin and other foreigners working and living in Japan?

[7]

Conclusion

Latin musical genres such as bossa nova, samba, tango, and salsa swept Japan in the 1970s.[1] Japan's samba boom has had its ups and downs, but since the 1980s, the number of samba aficionados in Japan has grown steadily, and *batucadas* (percussion ensembles) have sprung up in cities throughout the country. Many towns have sponsored or hosted yearly "carnivals" in which such bands paraded and entertained large crowds. The Asakusa carnival in the old downtown part of Tokyo started in the early 1980s and has grown to include more than two thousand participants, almost all of whom were Japanese. Regularly drawing more than four hundred thousand spectators, it has been one of Tokyo's most well attended festivals. The city of Kobe has had a yearly samba carnival that was even bigger. In addition, Brazilian performers have regularly toured Japanese cities, as have jazz and classical musicians, rock stars, and rappers from around the world, all feeding the voracious Japanese appetite for foreign cultural performances.

Much of the recent anthropology of globalization celebrates this kind of cultural flow (e.g. Appadurai 1990; Glick Schiller et al. 1992; Kearney 1995; Hannerz 1996a, 1996b). This flow results in creole cultures and multiethnic communities that make the claims to ethnic homogeneity and cultural par-

[1] Latin music first entered Japan much earlier than the 1970s. Marta Savigliano has written about an earlier entry of tango to aristocratic circles in Japan in the 1920s and '30s via Europe, in conjunction with a growing craze for ballroom dancing (1992, 235–52). The glossy Tokyo-based Latin music journal *Latina: Musica Contemporanea del Mundo* has been published monthly since the 1950s, with articles covering performances by South American musicians at clubs throughout Japan. The Japanese feature film *Shall We Dance?* (1996) indicates how widespread ballroom dancing forms of salsa, samba, rumba, and tango have become in contemporary Japan.

ticularism of nation-states such as Japan more difficult to sustain. In addition to the flow of such cultural forms as music, capital, and material goods, people have been moving at ever faster rates across international borders. Certainly new communication technologies and modes of transportation are making the world a smaller place. Anthony Giddens has suggested that new technologies and "expert systems" have freed people from the immediacies of local contexts and have expanded material and social environments (1990, 27).

But Japanese enthusiasm for foreign cultures has not been matched by an equivalent embrace of foreign workers. The flow of information, capital, commodities, and people across international borders has been subject to different degrees of government regulation, with international migration involving a change in membership from one putatively homogenous nation-state to another more restricted than any other flow (Zolberg 1990, 179). Even when people have been able to move farther and faster than ever, their immediate needs often can be satisfied only within the local communities where they live and work. Without membership within local communities, migrants may be excluded from health insurance, due process under law, and other rights taken for granted by citizens of many nation-states (see chapter 4). Even if governments are unable to control immigration completely, they have maintained stringent policies restricting the kinds of work migrants can perform, their length of stay, and the possibility of naturalization. In many ways, these policies determine the conditions under which migrant groups live and work.

Through a narrative of suffering and overcoming and through appeals to blood ties, Nikkeijin have been constructed and have constructed themselves as essentially Japanese (see chapter 2). If foreign labor was necessary for the Japanese economy, Nikkeijin were perceived to be a less threatening kind of foreigner, or not to be foreign at all. The undeniable linguistic and cultural differences of second- and third-generation Nikkeijin have surprised many Japanese workers, managers, and neighborhood residents who interacted with them for the first time. These interactions should not necessarily have led Japanese to reclassify Nikkeijin as more foreign than Japanese. The interactions could have led some Japanese in a more positive direction, to imagine more inclusive criteria for membership in Japanese society that would encompass those who were genealogically related yet culturally different, or even those who were considered genealogically unrelated yet linguistically and culturally fluent. Embodying cultural difference within what was construed as racial sameness, Nikkeijin could have motivated some Japanese to question their assumptions that race and culture naturally correlated with each other and that both were necessary criteria for being Japanese (see Linger 2001).

[139]

More commonly, however, interactions with Nikkeijin have led Japanese to invoke more exclusive, rather than inclusive, criteria for membership in Japanese society. The shock of cultural difference in itself cannot explain this outcome. We need to understand the role played by mediating institutions in determining the kinds of interactions encouraged between Japanese and Nikkeijin. Local social, political, and economic institutions have incorporated or channeled global flows of information, capital, goods, and people in specific ways. With regard to recent immigrants in the United States, Louise Lamphere has written that "mediating institutions" often serve to marginalize newcomers (1992). Throughout this book, I have tried to demonstrate some of the ways in which mediating institutions channeled cultural flows and patterned the hybrid cultural forms their intersection sometimes produced. In Hamamatsu, the illegal but tolerated system of employment brokers has played a decisive role in mediating relations between Japanese and Nikkeijin. This system, which has included not only brokers but also manufacturers and government agencies, has operated to segment and to differentiate Nikkeijin and Japanese from each other. Over time, each group has increasingly emphasized key cultural symbols in opposition to the other in a process that I call "oppositional florescence."

Marshall Sahlins has described how the Northwest Coast potlatch, Hawaiian chiefly pageantry, and the system of Chinese tribute and trade all experienced periods of highly embellished development or "florescence" in the face of supposedly overwhelming and homogenizing forces of Western capitalism (Sahlins 1988). In contrast, oppositional florescence involves a more conscious and strategic selection of cultural symbols in a historical context in which people have become self-conscious about culture and the politics of identity. In Hamamatsu, this manifested itself in Nikkeijin adoption of samba and soccer, and in the Brazilian flags that adorned almost any business catering primarily to Brazilian clientele. Members of the Brazilian culture center (see chapter 5) emphasized such markers of Brazilian identity even while they were considering staying permanently in Japan.

Edivaldo Kishimoto, the out-of-work geologist whom I had gotten to know well in Hamamatsu, expressed some of his frustration with working in a factory through a parodic embrace of a working-class identity. *"Sou bom trabalhador"* ("I'm a good worker/laborer"), he would joke, often adding that *"qualquer idiota"* (any idiot) could do the kind of work he was doing. His alienation at his factory also led Edivaldo to emphasize his Brazilian identity and simultaneously to cultivate relationships with certain Japanese outside the workplace. Edivaldo had made a significant effort to learn some Japanese, but he preferred to publicly emphasize a Brazilian identity; he chastised other Nikkeijin who mixed Japanese into their speech and who adopted other Japanese ways. He disdained the sentimental attachment to

Japan of those like his aunt who attended the Conference for Overseas Japanese (see chapter 2). Like other Nikkeijin, Edivaldo had gone to Japan with the notion that he was in some sense returning to roots and with the hope of discovering a culture more compatible than mainstream Brazilian culture. In reality, however, exclusion from meaningful social relationships with Japanese at work led Edivaldo and other Nikkeijin to identify with markers of Brazilian identity, such as samba, to which he and many Nikkeijin had previously been indifferent.

Likewise, among Japanese managers, workers, academics, and bureaucrats in Hamamatsu, oppositional florescence took the form of a revived discourse on Japanese values, especially the work ethic and responsibility, even as Japanese lifetime employment practices increasingly came under stress starting in the early 1990s (see chapter 3). These values reflected an idealized understanding of community as a group of people bound together by a strong sense of common purpose and mutual responsibility. In expressing this vision of community as distinctively Japanese, managers indirectly justified not only Nikkeijin marginalization in the employment system but also their exclusion from health insurance and, in many cases, from accident compensation (see chapter 4). Oppositional florescence in this case involved the intensification of certain preexisting practices or ideologies that allowed groups in contact to distinguish themselves from each other and, in this case, to justify inequality or exclusion.

Samba swept Japan in the 1970s. Yet only since the late 1980s have Brazilian people themselves—and primarily those of Japanese ancestry—been encouraged to migrate to Japan in large numbers. And although samba music was a craze, Nikkeijin have become known more as part of a larger "foreign worker problem" (gaikokujin rōdōsha mondai). Social scientists, bureaucrats, and others in Japan have tended to exaggerate the significance of cultural differences in the difficult relations of Japanese and Nikkeijin. Some have suggested that these differences could be reconciled through cultural understanding. Without denying the existence of significant cultural differences, I suggest that little progress can be made to ameliorate tensions between these groups without attending to the function of mediating institutions in stimulating oppositional florescence between them.

Pushing his baggage cart in front of him, Gilberto Honda emerged from the arrival gate at New York's John F. Kennedy International Airport. He looked much the same as he had when I last saw him four years earlier, in 1997, except that he had dyed his black hair the dull reddish brown common among Japanese youth. He was on his way back to Japan after spending three weeks in Brazil; he would be spending a day and a half with me in New York City and another five days with his cousins in Washington, D.C. Gilberto would be able to sport his youthfully dyed hair for the next week until he returned to Japan and had to conform to social norms at his work-place. He had been working at a factory, making air filters, for the past three years, and he said that his fondness for his boss, more than the threat of any formal sanction, made him feel pressure to conform.

Although I have emphasized oppositional florescence of Japanese and Nikkeijin in Japan, in some cases members of each group have accommodated each other. Gilberto told me that he had regularly worked four or five hours of overtime every day until he left for this most recent trip to Brazil. He had accommodated himself to life in Japan, and to some extent the Japanese he regularly came into contact with had accommodated him. Gilberto noted that his boss would never have been able to take a month off from work, although such lengthy leaves were granted to Nikkeijin who had proved to be steady workers over a year or more.

This was Gilberto's eleventh year in Japan. In addition to establishing good relationships at work, Gilberto had become ensconced within a social network of Brazilians and several Japanese. He still did not think in terms of settling in Japan permanently, but he had no intention of moving back to Brazil soon. The same was apparently true of Luís Horikawa, the head of the short-lived Brazilian culture center in Hamamatsu (see chapter 5). Gilberto told me that Luís was doing quite well now. He was working in a factory, and on weekends volunteered with a group formed by a Japanese Brazilian Catholic priest, providing food for homeless people (almost all Japanese) who congregated around the underpasses and parks in Hama-matsu's downtown area. Gilberto mentioned that Luís seemed more self-assured than he had been when I lived with him, and that he was dating a nice woman he had met at church.

If Luís had found a social as well as spiritual outlet within the Catholic Church and its volunteer activities in Japan, Antônia Narita, who had worked with Luís at the culture center, had found, in part through Gilberto, an alternative form of spiritual practice. She had moved back to Brazil in 1997, then again to Japan in 1998, and then back to Brazil again in 1999. When I met her in São Paulo during the summer of 2000 she was living with her sister in an apartment over her parents' grocery. She worked six days a week for one of the city's private bus lines and devoted most of her spare time to spiritual healing practices. When people came to her for consultation, she said, she would act as a medium, allowing herself to be possessed by her guardian angel, a deity from Mount Fuji, and other deities who could advise her clients. Antônia planned on returning to Japan in 2001 to continue her studies with Gilberto and his Japanese teacher.

Gilberto's interests in mysticism had grown in the years after his factory accident. He had developed a long-term relationship with a Japanese spiritual healer with whom he had made two short trips to China. On weekends,

Gilberto often worked with this healer to attend to the needs of Nikkeijin confronting a variety of problems—physical, psychological, financial, and romantic. People living in Hamamatsu, Nagoya, Gumma, and as far away as Toyama Prefecture visited their apartment for advice and treatment.

During the summer that I met Antônia in Brazil, I also visited my old friend Marcelo Matsumoto, whom I had known from my student days in Kobe. He had married a Brazilian of Italian descent and had two beautiful little girls. I had read in a newspaper about a Japanese mystic, Hirota Massatsugo, who ran a spiritual center *(terreno)* in the town of Atibáia, where Marcelo lived. Hirota regularly traveled to Japan, where hundreds of Nikkeijin would attend his sessions at various locations, including Hamamatsu. When Marcelo and I arrived at Hirota's center, we found a line of a hundred or so Nikkeijin waiting inside the compound by the main hall where the healer was to start consultations later in the morning. I had a hunch that at least some of those in line at Hirota's center had gone to Japan to work. I did not expect to meet anyone I knew there.

It took me only a moment to recognize the middle-aged woman's coarse voice calling my name from the line. It was Edivaldo Kishimoto's mother. Edivaldo and his parents had moved back to Brazil in 1998 after living in Japan for five years, and I remembered his mother well. Her gruff voice, jovial style of interaction, and creolized use of Japanese and Portuguese contrasted with the quiet Japanese style of her elder sister, with whom I had attended the Conference for Overseas Japanese (see chapter 2). I had been in touch with Edivaldo earlier in the summer so his parents knew I was in the area, but it was still a great surprise to meet each other at Hirota's spiritual center. Edivaldo's parents had gone there with his maternal grandparents, another of his aunts, and a cousin. I introduced them all to Marcelo. Edivaldo's mother told me that they had retired to a small town about four hours by bus from São Paulo where they built four houses—one for themselves and one for each of their three sons. I told them I had gotten a job and said that I had read about Hirota's spiritual center in the newspaper.

I did not accompany them as they went in for their consultations, but I spoke to them when they emerged, each with a bandage placed on a different part of his or her body. Edivaldo's mother had a bandage across the bridge of her nose for her sinus headaches. Edivaldo's cousin had a bandage just under her collarbone for high blood pressure. I did not notice any bandage on his father. A hint of embarrassment gave way to a mischievous glimmer in his eyes as he tugged downward on his belt, exposing the tip of a bandage, which, he indicated suggestively with his finger, was for impotence. "Would it work?" I asked, and they all laughed, adding that they didn't know, but that it didn't hurt to try. Despite their various ailments, the Kishimotos were in good spirits. Their trip to Hirota's center was not an expression of their alienation. It was, rather, a social occasion, an opportunity to see the countryside, to spend the day with their extended family, and to participate in activities that in some way symbolized their identity as Japanese Brazilians, which had been reinforced by their recent migration to and from Japan.

Edivaldo himself scoffed at the idea of visiting such a place, yet his parents felt that he needed direction and consultation more than any of them. He had long since given up the idea of continuing his career as a geologist; he had decided to earn a degree in education and to teach in primary or secondary schools. He shuttled back and forth between his house on the weekends and an aunt's apartment in São Paulo during the week to attend classes. His parents did not foresee him enjoying a career as a poorly paid teacher and asked me to do what I could to help find him opportunities in the United States. He had not maintained contact with many Nikkeijin friends from Hamamatsu but had developed a large number of "virtual friends" spread across Japan, Brazil, and other countries through Internet chat rooms for Nikkeijin.

Some Nikkeijin, like Edivaldo, have returned to Brazil, where they have had difficulty readjusting to Brazilian society. Others, like Antônia, have shuttled back and forth between Brazil and Japan, uncertain where to settle. Still others, like Gilberto and Luís, have been much more constant in their residence in Japan, where, to different degrees, they have carved out separate social places for themselves and have accommodated themselves to the broader society. Although Nikkeijin in Japan have not been able to choose where they would like to work as much as they could during the early 1990s, most still have found employment despite a long recession. The number of Nikkeijin residing in Japan in fact has continued slowly to grow, far surpassing 250,000 by 2001. They have continued to fill manufacturing and service sector jobs that insufficient numbers of Japanese were willing to fill at the wages being offered. The movement of manufacturing plants overseas will not necessarily reduce the demand for foreign labor for a reduction in manufacturing jobs is generally accompanied by an expansion of much lower paying service jobs, which are even less appealing for native workers (Sassen 1988). The low birthrate and rapid aging of the Japanese population suggests that foreign workers will become an increasingly important part of the workforce (Douglass and Roberts 2000).

What will multiethnic and multicultural Japan look like? The interactions of Japanese and Nikkeijin may provide some clues, as well as ideas for positive intervention. With or without a consensus in support of it, Japanese society is becoming increasingly multicultural. As the kite festival illustrated, certain kinds of positive interactions can evolve without government guidance (see chapter 6). Such cases, however, have been few and far between. Mediating institutions such as the employment system more often than not determine foreign workers' apparent cultural incompatibility with Japanese workplace communities. A more positive multicultural future depends at least in part on government policy that reforms such institutions.

Bibliography

Abegglen, James C. 1958. *The Japanese Factory: Aspects of Its Social Organization.* Glencoe, Ill.: Free Press.

Anderson, Benedict. 1991. *Imagined Communities: Reflections on the Origins and Spread of Nationalism.* 2nd ed. London: Verso.

Appadurai, Arjun. 1986. Introduction, *The Social Life of Things: Commodities in Cultural Perspective*, edited by A. Appadurai. Cambridge: Cambridge University Press.

——. 1990. "Disjuncture and Difference in the Global Cultural Economy." *Public Culture* 2, no. 2: 1–24.

Asahi Shimbun. 1996. *Japan Almanac 1997.* Asahi Shimbun.

Ashkenazi, Michael. 1993. *Matsuri: Festivals of a Japanese Town.* Honolulu: University of Hawaii Press.

Basch, Linda, Nina Glick Schiller, and Cristina Szanton Blanc. 1994. *Nations Unbound.* Australia [Langhorne, Pa.] Gordon and Breach Publishers.

Battaglia, Debbora. 1995. "On Practical Nostalgia: Self-Prospecting among Urban Trobrianders." In *Rhetorics of Self-Making*, edited by Debbora Battaglia. Berkeley: University of California Press.

Baumann, Gerd. 1992. "Ritual Implicates 'Others': Rereading Durkheim in a Plural Society." In *Understanding Rituals*, edited by Daniel de Coppet. London: Routledge.

Bestor, Theodore. 1989. *Neighborhood Tokyo.* Stanford: Stanford University Press.

——. 1992. "Conflict, Legitimacy, and Tradition in a Tokyo Neighborhood." In *Japanese Social Organization*, edited by Takie Sugiyama Lebra. Honolulu: University of Hawaii Press.

——. 1993. "Rediscovering Shitamachi: Subculture, Class, and Tokyo's 'Traditional' Urbanism." In *The Cultural Meaning of Urban Space*, edited by Robert Rotenberg and Gary McDonogh. Westport, Ct.: Bergin & Garvey.

Bonacich, Edna, and John Modell. 1980. *The Economic Basis of Ethnic Solidarity.* Berkeley: University of California Press.

[147]

Bornstein, Lisa. 1992. "From *Carioca* to *Karaoke*: Brazilian Guestworkers in Japan." *Berkeley Planning Journal* 27: 48–75.

Bourgois, Philippe I. 1989. *Ethnicity at Work: Divided Labor on a Central American Banana Plantation*. Baltimore: Johns Hopkins University Press.

Breytenbach, Breyten. 1991. "The Long March from Hearth to Heart." *Social Research: an International Quarterly of Social Sciences* 58, no. 1: 69–83.

Brinton, Mary C. 1992. "Christmas Cakes and Wedding Cakes: Gender and Work in Postwar Japan." In *Japanese Social Organization*, edited by Takie Sugiyama Lebra. Honolulu: University of Hawaii Press.

Burajiru Nihon Imin Hachijūnen Shi Hensan I'inkai. 1991. *Burajiru Nihon Imin Hachijūnen Shi* [The 80 Year History of Japanese Immigration to Brazil]. São Paulo: Burajiru Nihon Bunka Kyōkai.

Centro de Estudos Nipo-Brasileiros. 1990. *Pesquisa da População de Descendentes de Japoneses Residentes no Brasil*. São Paulo: Centro de Estudos Nipo-Brasileiros.

Chan, Sucheng. 1991. *Asian Americans: An Interpretive History*. New York: Twayne Publishers.

Comaroff, John. 1987. "Of Totemism and Ethnicity: Consciousness, Practice, and the Signs of Inequality." *Ethnos* 52: 301–23.

DaMatta, Roberto. 1991 [1979]. *Carnivals, Rogues, and Heroes: An Interpretation of the Brazilian Dilemma*. Translated by John Drury. Notre Dame: University of Notre Dame Press.

Davis, Winston. 1980. *Dojo: Magic and Exorcism in Modern Japan*. Stanford: Stanford University Press.

di Leonardo, Micaela. 1984. *The Varieties of Ethnic Experience: Kinship, Class, and Gender among California Italian-Americans*. Ithaca: Cornell University Press.

Dore, Ronald. 1973. *British Factory—Japanese Factory: The Origins of National Diversity in Industrial Relations*. Berkeley: University of California Press.

——. 1987. "Goodwill and the Spirit of Market Capitalism." In *Taking Japan Seriously: A Confucian Perspective on Leading Economic Issues*, by R. Dore. Stanford: Stanford University Press.

Douglass, Mike, and Glenda S. Roberts, eds. 2000. *Japan and Global Migration: Foreign Workers and the Advent of a Multicultural Society*. London: Routledge.

Espiritu, Yen Le. 1992. *Asian American Panethnicity: Bridging Institutions and Identities*. Philadelphia: Temple University Press.

Fuchigami Eiji. 1995. *Nikkeijin Shōmei—Nanbei Imin, Nihon e no Dekasegi no Kōzu* [Nikkeijin Testament: Migrants to South America, and the Composition of Migrant Work to Japan]. Tokyo: Shinhyōron.

Fujitani, Takashi. 1996. *Splendid Monarchy: Power and Pageantry in Modern Japan*. Berkeley: University of California Press.

Giddens, Anthony. 1990. *The Consequences of Modernity*. Stanford: Stanford University Press.

Glick Schiller, Nina, Linda Basch, and Cristina Blanc-Szanton. 1992. *Towards a Transnational Perspective on Migration: Race, Class, Ethnicity, and Nationalism Reconsidered*. Annals of the New York Academy of Sciences, v. 645. New York: New York Academy of Sciences.

Gluckman, Max. 1963. *Order and Rebellion in Tribal Africa*. New York: Free Press of Glencoe.

Gordon, Andrew. 1985. *The Evolution of Labor Relations in Japan: Heavy Industry, 1853–1955*. Harvard East Asian Monographs, 117. Council on East Asian Studies, Harvard University.

Greenwood, Davydd J., William Foote Whyte, and Ira Harkavy. 1993. "Participatory Action Research as a Process and a Goal." *Human Relations* 46, no. 2: 175–92.

Haley, John O. 1986. "Comment: The Implications of Apology." *Law & Society Review* 20, no. 4: 499–508.

Hamamatsu-shi. 1995a. "Gaikokujin Tōroku Kokusekibetsu Jinin Chōsahyō" [Table of Aggregate Numbers of Registered Foreigners by Nationality].

———. 1995b. *Dai 56–kai Hamamatsu-shi Tōkei-sho* [Hamamatsu-shi Statistics]. Heisei 7–nen ban.

Hamamatsu-shi Kankō Konbenshon-ka [Hamamatsu City Tourism and Conventions Division]. *Hamamatsu Matsuri. 1996*.

Hamamatsu-shi Kokusai Kōryū Shitsu [Hamamatsu City International Exchange Office]. March 1997. *Nikkeijin no Seikatsu Jittai Ishiki Chōsa* [Survey of Actual Living Conditions and Consciousness of Overseas Japanese].

Handa, Tomoo. 1980. *Memórias de um Imigrante Japonês no Brasil* [Memories of a Japanese Immigrant in Brazil]. Translated from Japanese by Antonio Nojiri. São Paulo: Centro de Estudos Nipo-Brasileiros.

Hannerz, Ulf. 1996a [1994]. "The Global Ecumene as a Landscape of Modernity." In *Transnational Connections*, chapter 4. London: Routledge.

———. 1996b [1995]. "The Local and the Global." In *Transnational Connections*, chapter 2.

Hello Work (Hamamatsu Kōkyū Shokugyō Anteisho). 1995. "Heisei 7–nen Gaikokujin Koyō Jokyō Hokoku Shūkei Kekka" [1995 Foreigners' Employment Conditions].

Herzfeld, Michael. 1992. *The Social Production of Indifference: Exploring the Symbolic Roots of Western Bureaucracy*. Chicago: University of Chicago Press.

Higuchi Naoto. 1998. "Zainichi Burajirujin to Nikkei Shinshūkyō" [Brazilians in Japan and Nikkei New Religions]. *Hitotsubashi Kenkyū* [Hitotsubashi University Research] 23, no. 1: 161–73.

Higuchi Naoto and Takahashi Sachie. 1998a. "Esunikku Sabukarutyā kara Shimin Sanka e?" [From Ethnic Subculture to Citizen Participation?] *Nempō Shakaigaku Ronshū* [Annual Review of Sociology] no. 11 (June): 83–94.

———. 1998b. "Zainichi Burajiru Shusshinsha no Esunikku Bijinesu" [Ethnic Business of Brazilians in Japan]. *Ibero Amerika Kenkyū* [Iberian American Research] 20, no. 1: 1–15.

Hook, Glenn D., and Michael A. Weiner, eds. 1992. *The Internationalization of Japan*. London: Routledge.

Hōsei Daigaku Ōhara Shakai Mondai Kenkyūsho. "Dai 62–shu Nihon rōdō nenban [62nd Annual Report of Japanese Labor]." 1992.

Hosokawa Shūhei. 1995. *Samba no Kuni ni Enka ga Nagareru: Ongaku ni Miru Nikkei Burajiru Iminshi* [The Sounds of Enka in the Country of Samba: Nikkei Brazilian Migration History as Seen Through Music]. Chūkō Shinsho 1263. Tokyo: Chūō Kōron-sha.

———. 1999. *Shinemaya, Burajiru o Iku: Nikkei Imin no Kyōshū to Aidenteitei* [Cinema Theater Goes to Brazil: Nostalgia and Identity among Nikkei Migrants]. Tokyo: Shinchōsha.

Bibliography

Ikegami Noriaki. 1997. "Seikatsu-sha toshite no Nyūkamā to Chiiki Shakai: Hama-matsu-shi ni okeru Kōkyō Sābisu o Megutte" [Resident Newcomers and Regional Society: Hamamatsu City Public Services]. Shizuoka Kenritsu Daigaku Tanki Daigakubu.

Isaacs, Harold R. 1975. "Basic Group Identity: The Idols of the Tribe." In *Ethnicity: Theory and Experience*, edited by Nathan Glazer and Daniel P. Moynihan. Cambridge: Harvard University Press.

Ishi, Angelo. 1994. "Quem é Quem no Tribunal da Discriminação?" [Who's Who in the Tribunal of Discrimination?] In *A Quebra dos Mitos: O Fenômeno Dekassegui através de Relatos Pessoais* [Undermining Myths: The Dekasegi Phenomenon through Personal Accounts], edited by Charles Tetsuo Chigusa. Atsugi, Japan: International Press Corporation.

———. 1995. "Nikkei Burajirujin Dekasegi Rōdōsha to Shūkyō" [Japanese-descendant Brazilian Workers and Religion]. In *Dekasegi Nikkei Burajiru-jin* vol. 1 [Japanese Brazilian Migrant Workers], edited by Watanabe Masako. Tokyo: Akashi Shoten.

———. 1996. "Dekasegi Keikensha no Manga kara Hanshin Daishinsai Hōdō made: Porutogarugo Media no Kaishingeki" [Dekasegi Veterans from Their Cartoons to the Coverage of the Kobe Earthquake: The Remarkable Advance of the Portuguese Language Media]. In *Esunikku Media: Tabunka Nihon e* [Ethnic Media: Towards a Multicultural Japan], edited by Shiramizu Shigehiko, chapter 5. Tokyo: Akashi Shoten.

Ivy, Marilyn. 1988. "Tradition and Difference in Japanese Mass Media." *Public Culture* 1, no. 1: 21–30.

———. 1995. *Discourses of the Vanishing: Modernity, Phantasm, Japan*. Chicago: University of Chicago Press.

Kaigai Nikkeijin Kyōkai. 1997. "Nikkeijin Hompō Shūrōsha Dōkō Chōsa Hokokusho" [Survey Results of Nikkeijin Workers' Trends in Our Country].

Kearney, Michael. 1995. "The Local and the Global: The Anthropology and Transnationalism." *Annual Review of Anthropology* 24: 547–65.

Kelly, William. 1993. "Finding a Place in Metropolitan Japan: Ideologies, Institutions, and Everyday Life." In *Postwar Japan as History*, edited by Andrew Gordon. Berkeley: University of California Press.

Kitagawa Toyoie. March 1993. "Hamamatsu-shi ni okeru Gaikokujin no Seikatsu Jittai Ishiki Chōsa" [Survey of Foreign Workers in Hamamatsu]. Hamamatsu-shi kikakubu kokusai kōryū shitsu.

Knight, John. 1993. "Rural *kokusaika*? Foreign Motifs and Village Revival in Japan." *Japan Forum* 5, no. 2: 203–16.

Koike, Kazuo. 1983. "Internal Labor Markets: Workers in Large Firms." In *Contemporary Industrial Relations in Japan*, edited by Taishiro Shirai. Madison: University of Wisconsin Press.

Koike Seiji. 1981. "Takoage-kai no Zengo" [On the subject of the kite flying committee]. *Tōmi Kenkyū* no. 5: 38–54.

Kokusai Kyōryoku Jigyōdan [Japan International Cooperation Agency (JICA)]. 1992. "Nikkeijin Hompō Shūrōsha Dōkō Chōsa Hōkokusho" [Survey Results of Nikkeijin Workers' Trends in Our Country]. Gyōmu Shiryō no. 854.

Komai, Hiroshi. 1995 [1993]. *Migrant Workers in Japan*. Translated by Jens Wilkinson. London: Kegan Paul International.

Kondo, Dorinne. 1990. *Crafting Selves*. Chicago: University of Chicago Press.

Kumazawa, Makoto. 1996. *Portraits of the Japanese Workplace: Labor Movements, Workers, and Mangers*. Translated by Andrew Gordon and Mikiso Hane. Boulder, Colo.: Westview Press.

LaFleur, William. 1992. *Liquid Life: Abortion and Buddhism in Contemporary Japan*. Princeton: Princeton University Press.

Lamphere, Louise. 1992. "Introduction: The Shaping of Diversity." In *Structuring Diversity: Ethnographic Perspectives on the New Immigration*, edited by Louise Lamphere. Chicago: University of Chicago Press.

Lesser, Jeffrey. 1999. *Negotiating National Identity: Immigrants, Minorities, and the Struggle for Ethnicity in Brazil*. Durham: Duke University Press.

Lie, John. 2001. *Multiethnic Japan*. Cambridge: Harvard University Press.

Limón, José. 1994. *Dancing with the Devil: Society and Cultural Poetics in Mexican-American South Texas*. Madison: University of Wisconsin Press.

Linger, Daniel. 1992. *Dangerous Encounters: Meanings of Violence in a Brazilian City*. Stanford: Stanford University Press.

———. 2001. *No One Home*. Stanford: Stanford University Press.

Maeyama Takashi. 1972. "Ancestor, Emperor, and Immigrant: Religious and Group Identification of the Japanese in Rural Brazil (1908–50)." *Journal of Interamerican Studies and World Affairs* 14, no. 2: 151–82.

———. 1981. *Hisōzokusha no Seishinshi* [Spiritual History of Non-Successors]. Tokyo: Ochanomizu Shobō.

———. 1982. *Imin no Nihon Kaiki Undō* [Japanese Immigrants' Repatriation Movement]. Tokyo: Nihon Hōsō Shuppan Kyōkai.

———. 1983. "Japanese Religions in Southern Brazil: Change and Syncretism." *Latin American Studies* (University of Tsukuba, Ibaraki, Japan) 6: 181–238.

———. 1996a [1979]. "Nikkeijin to Nihon Bunka—Toku ni Nikkei Burajiru Bunka to Kokka-kan ni tsuite" [Nikkeijin and Japanese Culture: Especially in Relation to Japanese Brazilian Culture and National Perspective]. In *Esunishitei to Burajiru Nikkeijin—Bunka Jinruigaku teki Kenkyū* [Ethnicity and Japanese Brazilians: Cultural Anthropological Research]. Tokyo: Ochanomizu Shobō.

———. 1996b [1982]. "Aidenteitei to Tekiō Sutoratejii—Sono Rekishiteki Hensen" [Identity and Adaptation Strategy: Their Historical Transformations]. In *Esunishitei to Burajiru Nikkeijin*.

———. 1996c [1984]. "Nikkeijin no Wakon Hakusai Ron—'Akarutyureesyon' ni tsuite no Ichi Minyō Gainen" [The Discourse on Japanese Spirit and Brazilian Learning: One Folk Concept of 'Acculturation']. In *Esunishitei to Burajiru Nikkeijin*.

———. 1996d [1987]. "Ibunka Sesshoku to Bunka Hendō" [Contact between Different Cultures and Cultural Change]. In *Esunishitei to Burajiru Nikkeijin*.

———. 1997. *Ihō ni "Nihon" o Matsuru: Burajiru Nikkeijin no Shūkyō to Esunishitei*. Tokyo: Ochanomizu Shobō.

Maniwa Mitsuyuki. 1997. *Wagakuni no Kokusaika ni tomonau Bunkateki, Kaisōteki Masatsu to Juyō Taisei no Shakaigakuteki Chōsa Kenkyū—Shizuoka-ken o Chūshin ni* [Survey Research of the System of Cultural and Class Friction and Acceptance—Centering on Shizuoka Prefecture]. Shizuoka: Shizuoka Daigaku Jinbungakubu Shakaigaku Kenkyūshitsu.

McConnell, David. 2000. *Importing Diversity: Inside Japan's JET Program*. Berkeley: University of California Press.

Miyajima Takashi and Higuchi Naoto. 1996. "Iryō, Shakai Hoshō: Sonzai-ken no Kan-ten kara" [Medical Care and Social Insurance: from the Perspective of the Rights of Residence]. In *Gaikokujin Rodosha kara Shimin e* [From Foreign Workers to Residents], edited by Miyajima Takashi and Kajita Takamichi. Tokyo: Yuhikaku.

Miyajima Takashi and Kajita Takamichi, eds. 1996. *Gaikokujin Rodosha kara Shimin e* [From Foreign Workers to Residents]. Tokyo: Yuhikaku.

Monna Kunio. March 1993. "Hōki Sareru Koyō Sekinin: Haken Gyōsha o Nakushitai" [Employment Responsibility Discarded: Wanting To Do Away with Labor Brokers]. *Impaction* 79: 58–63.

———. Nov. 1993. "200–nin no 'Tamatsuki' Kaiko Jiken" [200-Person Billiard Ball Lay-off Incident]. *Hamamatsu Overseas Labourers Solidarity (HLS no kai) Newsletter* no. 41.

———. May 1994. "Shigatsu kara mo Kokumin Kenkō Hoken ni Haireruyo" [Enroll-ment in National Health Insurance Still Possible in April] *Hamamatsu Overseas Labourers Solidarity (HLS no kai) Newsletter no. 45.*

———. Oct. 1995, Jan. 1996, Feb. 1996. "Kaiko tte Ittai Nani?" I, II, III [How on Earth Is 'To Be Laid Off' Being Defined? Parts I, II, III]. *HLS newsletter* no. 57, 60, 61.

Murakami Yasusuke and Thomas P. Rohlen. 1992. "Social-exchange Aspects of the Japanese Political Economy: Culture, Efficiency, and Change." In *The Political Economy of Japan*, vol. 3, edited by Shumpei Kumon and Henry Rosovsky. Stan-ford: Stanford University Press.

Nelson, John. 1996. *A Year in the Life of a Shinto Shrine*. Seattle: University of Wash-ington Press.

Nishiyama, Tsuyoshi. 1994. *Tokyo no Kyababu no Kemuri* [Tokyo Kebab Smoke]. Tokyo: Keishobō.

Nolte, Sharon, and Sally Hastings. 1991. "Meiji State's Policy toward Women, 1890–1910." In *Recreating Japanese Women, 1600–1945*, edited by Gail Lee Bern-stein. Berkeley: University of California Press.

Nomura Masami. 1994. *Shūshin Koyō* [Lifetime Employment]. Dō-jidai raiburari no. 204. Tokyo: Iwanami Shoten.

North, Robert Scott. 1994. *Karōshi and the Politics of Workers' Compensation in Japan*. Master's thesis, University of Hawaii.

Ogasawara, Yuko. 1998. *Office Ladies and Salaried Men: Power, Gender, and Work in Japanese Companies*. Berkeley: University of California Press.

Okuda Michihiro and Junko Tajima, editors. 1991. *Ikebukuro no Ajiakei Gaikokujin* [Ikebukuro's Asian Foreigners]. Tokyo: Mekon.

———. 1993. *Shinjuku no Ajiakei Gaikokujin* [Shinjuku's Asian Foreigners]. Tokyo: Mekon.

Piore, Michael. 1979. *Birds of Passage: Migrant Labor and Industrial Societies*. Cam-bridge: Cambridge University Press.

Powell, Margaret, and Masahira Anesaki. 1990. *Health Care in Japan*. London: Rout-ledge.

Roberson, James E. 1998. *Japanese Working Class Lives: An Ethnographic Study of Factory Workers*. London: Routledge.

Roberts, Glenda. 1994. *Staying on the Line: Blue Collar Women in Contemporary Japan*. Honolulu: University of Hawaii Press.

———. 1996. "Careers and Commitment: Azumi's Blue-Collar Women." In *Reimaging Japanese Women*, edited by Anne Imamura. Berkeley: University of California Press.

Robertson, Jennifer. 1991. *Native and Newcomer: Making and Remaking a Japanese City*. Berkeley: University of California Press.

——. 1997. "Empire of Nostalgia: Rethinking 'Internationalization' in Japan Today." *Theory, Culture, and Society* 14, no. 4: 97–122.

Rōdōshō Rōdō Kijunkyoku [Ministry of Labor, Labor Standards Bureau]. 1992. *Rōdō Kijun Kantoku Nenpō* [Annual report of labor standards inspection], vol. 45.

Rohlen, Thomas P. 1974. *For Harmony and Strength: Japanese White-collar Organization in Anthropological Perspective*. Berkeley: University of California Press.

Roth, Joshua Hotaka. Forthcoming. "The Meaning of Overseas Voting Rights: Ambiguous Identifications among Elderly Japanese Migrants to Brazil." In *Searching for Home Abroad: Japanese Brazilians and the Transnational Moment*, edited by Jeffrey Lesser.

Sahlins, Marshall. 1988. "Cosmologies of Capitalism: the Trans-Pacific Sector of 'The World System.'" *Proceedings of the British Academy* 74: 1–51.

Sai Media Kenkyūkai. 1995. *Dekassegui—os Exilados Econômicos: A Realização de um Sonho* [Dekasegi—the Economic Exiles: The Realization of a Dream]. Tokyo: Kashiwa Shōbō.

Sakai, Naoki. 1991. "Return to the West/Return to the East: Watsuji Tetsuro's Anthropology and Discussions of Authenticity." *Boundary 2* 18, no. 3: 157–90.

Sassen, Saskia. 1988. *The Mobility of Labor and Capital: A Study in International Investment and Labor Flow*. Cambridge: Cambridge University Press.

Savigliano, Marta E. 1992. "Tango in Japan and the World Economy of Passion." In *Remade in Japan: Everyday Life and Consumer Taste in a Changing Society*. New Haven: Yale University Press.

Saxton, Alexander. 1971. *The Indispensable Enemy: Labor and the Anti-Chinese Movement in California*. Berkeley: University of California Press.

Schnell, Scott. 1999. *The Rousing Drum: Ritual Practice in a Japanese Community*. Honolulu: University of Hawaii Press.

Seidensticker, Edward. 1983. *Low City, High City: Tokyo from Edo to the Earthquake: How the Shogun's Ancient Capital Became a Great Modern City, 1867–1923*. Rutland, Vt., and Tokyo: Charles E. Tuttle Co.

Sellek, Yoko. 1997. "Nikkeijin: the Phenomenon of Return Migration." In *Japan's Minorities: The Illusion of Homogeneity*, edited by Michael Weiner. London: Routledge.

Shimada, Haruo. 1994. *Japan's Guest Workers: Issues and Public Policies*. Translated by Roger Northridge. Tokyo: University of Tokyo Press.

Shimizu Shigehiro. 1997. "Nikkei-Burajirujin no Esunikku Aidentitī Henyō" [Changing Ethnic Identity of Japanese Brazilians]. In *Wagakuni no Kokusaika ni Tomonau Bunkateki, Kaisōteki Masatsu to Juyō Taisei no Shakaigakuteki Chōsa Kenkyū— Shizuoka-ken o Chūshin ni* [Survey Research of the System of Cultural and Class Friction and Acceptance—Centering on Shizuoka Prefecture], edited by Maniwa Mitsuyuki. Shizuoka: Shizuoka Daigaku Jinbungakubu Shakaigaku Kenkyūshitsu.

Smith, Robert J. 1960. "Pre-Industrial Urbanism in Japan: A Consideration of Multiple Traditions in a Feudal Society." *Economic Development and Cultural Change* 9 (i.II): 241–57.

——. 1979. "The Ethnic Japanese in Brazil." *The Journal of Japanese Studies* 5, no. 1: 53–70.

Smith, Robert J., John B. Cornell, Hiroshi Saito, and Takashi Maeyama, eds. 1967. *The Japanese and Their Descendants in Brazil: An Annotated Bibliography*. São Paulo: Centro de Estudos Nipo-Brasileiros.

Smith, Thomas C. 1988. "The Right to Benevolence: Dignity and Japanese Workers, 1889–1920." In *Native Sources of Japanese Industrialization*. Berkeley: University of California Press.

Staniford, Philip. 1973. *Pioneers in the Tropics: The Political Organization of Japanese in an Immigrant Community in Brazil*. London School of Economics Monographs on Social Anthropology, no. 45. London: Athlone Press.

Stewart, Charles, and Rosalind Shaw, eds. 1994. *Syncretism/Anti-syncretism: The Politics of Religious Synthesis*. London: Routledge.

Takagi Hiroshi. 1993. "Fashizumuki, Ainu minzoku no Dōkaron" [Debates Concerning the Assimilation of the Ainu during the Fascist Period]. In *Bunka to Fashizumu: Senjika Nihon ni okeru Bunka no Kōbō* [Culture and Fascism: The Light of Culture during Wartime Japan], edited by Akazawa Shirō and Kitagawa Kenzō, 247–83. Tokyo: Nihon Keizai Hyōronsha.

Takahashi Hidemine. 1995. *Nise Nipponjin Tambōki—Kaette Kita Nambei Nikkeijintachi* [Record of the Search for Fake Japanese: Returned South American Nikkeijin]. Tokyo: Sōshisha.

Takaki, Ronald. 1989. *Strangers from a Different Shore: A History of Asian Americans*. Boston: Little, Brown.

Tanaka Hiroshi. 1991. *Zainichi Gaikokujin* [Foreigners in Japan]. Iwanami Shinsho no. 370. Tokyo: Iwanami Shoten.

Tanase, Takao. 1990. "The Management of Disputes: Automobile Accident Compensation in Japan." In *Law and Society Review* 24, no. 3: 650–89.

Taussig, Michael T. 1980. *The Devil and Commodity Fetishism in South America*. Chapel Hill: University of North Carolina Press.

Tezuka Kazuaki. 1995. *Gaikokujin to Hō* [Foreigners and the Law]. Tokyo: Yūhikaku.

Tsuda, Takeyuki. 1996. *Strangers in the Ethnic Homeland: The Migration, Ethnic Identity, and Psychosocial Adaptation of Japan's New Immigrant Minority*. Doctoral dissertation. Department of Anthropology, University of California at Berkeley.

———. 1998. "The Stigma of Ethnic Difference: The Structure of Prejudice and 'Discrimination' Towards Japan's New Immigrant Minority." *Journal of Japanese Studies* 24, no. 2: 317–59.

———. 1999. "The Permanence of 'Temporary' Migration: The 'Structural Embeddedness' of Japanese Brazilian Migrant Workers in Japan." *Journal of Asian Studies* 58, no. 3: 687–722.

———. 2000. "Acting Brazilian in Japan: Ethnic Resistance among Return Migrants." *Ethnology* 39, no. 1: 55–71.

Turner, Christena. 1991. "The Spirit of Productivity: Workplace Discourse on Culture and Economics in Japan." *Boundary 2* 18, no. 3: 90–105.

———. 1995. *Japanese Workers in Protest: An Ethnography of Consciousness and Experience*. Berkeley: University of California Press.

Turner, Victor. 1974. *Dramas, Fields, and Metaphors: Symbolic Action in Human Society*. Ithaca: Cornell University Press.

Upham, Frank. 1987. *Law and Social Change in Postwar Japan*. Cambridge: Harvard University Press.

Ventura, Rey. 1992. *Underground in Japan*. London: Jonathan Cape.

Vizentini, Paulo. 1998. "Brazil-Asia Relations and Their Perspectives." *International Institute for Asian Studies Newsletter* no. 16 (summer).

Vogel, Ezra F. 1971 [1963]. *Japan's New Middle Class: the Salary Man and His Family in a Tokyo Suburb*, 2nd ed. Berkeley: University of California Press.

Wagatsuma, Hiroshi, and Arthur Rosett. 1986. "The Implications of Apology: Law and Culture in Japan and the United States." *Law & Society Review* 20, no. 4: 461–98.

Wakatsuki Yasuo and Suzuki Joji. 1975. *Kaigai Ijū Seisakushi-ron* [History of Emigration Policy]. Tokyo: Fukumura Shuppan.

Watanabe Masako. 1995. "Nikkei Burajiru-jin no Koyō o Meguru Mondai" [Problems Faced in Hiring Japanese Brazilians]. In *Dekasegi Nikkei Burajiru-jin Vol. 1*, [Japanese Brazilian Migrant Workers], edited by Watanabe Masako. Tokyo: Akashi Shoten.

Weiner, Myron, and Tadashi Hanami, eds. 1998. *Temporary Workers or Future Citizens? Japanese and U.S. Migration Policies*. New York: New York University Press.

Yamanaka, Keiko. 2000. "'I Will Go Home, but When?': Labor Migration and Circular Diaspora Formation by Japanese Brazilians in Japan." In *Japan and Global Migration: Foreign Workers and the Advent of a Multicultural Society*, edited by Mike Douglass and Glenda S. Roberts. London: Routledge.

Yamashita, Karen. 1992. *Brazil Maru: A Novel*. Minneapolis: Coffee House Press.

———. 2001. *Circle K Cycles*. Minneapolis: Coffee House Press.

Yoneda Kazuo. 1986. "Shinsetsu Sahase Jingoro" [New Interpretation of Sahase Jingoro]. *Tōmi Kenkyū* no. 9 (March): 1–27.

Zolberg, Aristide. 1990. "Stranger Encounters." In *Les Etrangers dans la Ville: Le Regard des Sciences Sociales*, edited by Ida Simon-Barouch and Pierre-Jean Simon. Paris: Editions L'Harmattan.

Index

The Anthropology of Contemporary Issues

A SERIES EDITED
BY ROGER SANJEK

Rum and Axes: The Rise of a Connecticut Merchant Family, 1795–1850
    by Janet Siskind
History and Power in the Study of Law: New Directions in Legal Anthropology
    edited by June Starr and Jane F. Collier
"Getting Paid": Youth Crime and Work in the Inner City
    by Mercer L. Sullivan
Breaking the Silence: Redress and Japanese American Ethnicity
    by Yasuko I. Takezawa
Underground Harmonies: Music and Politics in the Subways of New York
    by Susie J. Tanenbaum
Generations in Touch: Linking the Old and Young in a Tokyo Neighborhood
    by Leng Leng Thang
City of Green Benches: Growing Old in a New Downtown
    by Maria D. Vesperi
Strawberry Fields: Politics, Class, and Work in California Agriculture
    by Miriam J. Wells
Renunciation and Reformation: A Study of Conversion in an American Sect
    by Harriet Whitehead
Upscaling Downtown: Stalled Gentrification in Washington, D. C.
    by Brett Williams
Women's Work and Chicano Families: Cannery Workers of the Santa Clara Valley
    by Patricia Zavella